NORTH
MC

NORTH AND EAST AREA

WALKS FOR MOTORISTS

Douglas Cossar
and
Geoffrey White

30 Walks with sketch maps

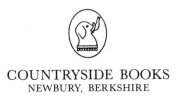

COUNTRYSIDE BOOKS
NEWBURY, BERKSHIRE

*Countryside Books' walking guides cover most areas of England
and Wales and include the following series:*

*County Rambles
Walks For Motorists
Exploring Long Distance Paths
Literary Walks
Pub Walks*

A complete list is available from the publisher.

First published by Frederick Warne Ltd

This edition published 1995

COUNTRYSIDE BOOKS
3 Catherine Road
Newbury, Berkshire

ISBN 1 85306 216 2

Cover photograph of Robin Hood's Bay from Ravenscar

Publishers' Note

At the time of publication all footpaths used in these walks were designated as official footpaths or rights of way, but it should be borne in mind that diversion orders may be made from time to time.

Although every care has been taken in the preparation of this Guide, neither the Author nor the Publisher can accept responsibility for those who stray from the Rights of Way.

Produced through MRM Associates Ltd., Reading
Typeset by Paragon Typesetters, Queensferry, Clwyd
Printed by J. W. Arrowsmith Ltd., Bristol

Contents

Preface

Here now is the complete revision of the second volume of Geoffrey White's *North York Moors Walks for Motorists*, which again I hope will be considered a worthy successor. The countryside covered has just as much to offer to the rambler, indeed the quality of the walking would be hard to better anywhere, but the accents as one moves north and east are a little different. The Forestry Commission own large tracts of land, so there are many walks in woodland, and one must compliment the Commission on the facilities they have provided for walkers: parking places and picnic sites, waymarked walks, viewpoints and information centres, and hope that threats of privatisation have now finally been averted. If not, much fine walking could be lost, and much of the present book would have to be re-written! Then there is the lovely Esk valley, with a wealth of beauty both to north and south, and the valleys of its tributary becks. And the North Yorkshire Moors Railway which, passing through glorious landscapes, is invaluable to walkers. Finally there is the coast, which some may feel gets a rather raw deal here, but as the clifftop paths hardly need any introduction I felt it more appropriate to concentrate on some of the less well-known paths inland.

Again, and for the same reasons that I mentioned in the previous volume, I have had to make many more changes to the original than I at first thought would be necessary. The aim was always to provide enjoyable walks for the family rambler, clearly described and with a minimum of navigational difficulty. All the routes are on rights of way or permissive paths (particularly through Forestry Commission plantations) or on paths where access has traditionally not been disputed. Please let me know, through the publishers, of any problems you may encounter, and do please report any obstructions, etc to the National Park Authority, The Old Vicarage, Bondgate, Helmsley, York YO6 5BP. I am very grateful to the National Park Area Rangers for reading the manuscript of this book and commenting on it: however the responsibility for any deficiencies in the text is of course mine.

Douglas Cossar
February 1995

4

Introduction

The North York Moors are a well-defined area of upland, roughly 60 kilometres from west to east and 40 from north to south, bounded on the east by the North Sea, on the north and west by the steep escarpments of the Cleveland and Hambleton Hills and on the south by the gentler dip slopes of the Tabular Hills. The area is dissected by a number of south-flowing streams draining into the Derwent, which flows into the Ouse, and in the north the Esk flows east to reach the sea at Whitby, being joined from the south by smaller becks.

Most of the moorland is sandstone, with occasional caps of gritstone on the highest hills. To the south these rocks are overlaid with Corallian limestone, forming the Tabular Hills, flat-topped with a scarp to the north and gentler slopes to the south. Among the sandstone strata are thin seams of poor-quality coal, and earlier rocks below contain deposits of iron ore, jet and alum, all of which have been exploited by man, most fully in the 19th century.

The infertile soils on the sandstone now form the largest continuous area of heather moorland in England, with land use restricted to sheep pasture and grouse shooting, but arable crops are grown on the limestone plateau and there is dairy farming in the valley bottoms. Since 1920 the Forestry Commission have added extensive plantations, mainly of conifers, to the remains of the earlier deciduous forest.

The hand of man is everywhere visible, from the many Bronze Age burial mounds through the medieval monasteries and crosses to the relics of industrial activity and the delightful stone-built, red pantile roofed villages and farmsteads of today.

All this variety makes the North York Moors into a paradise for walkers, naturalists, photographers, archaeologists, historians and many others. I have tried in the rambles to provide a reasonable selection of the various delights the area has to offer, in the hope that they will be a springboard for many more expeditions of independent exploration.

The best general map of the area is probably the Ordnance Survey's Touring Map No 2 at a scale of 1″ to the mile, but for the walker the essential maps are the Ordnance Survey's Outdoor Leisure Maps Nos 26 and 27 at a scale of 1:25 000; of the walks in this volume numbers 24, 25, 26, 28, 29 and 30 are on No 26, the Western sheet, all the others are on No 27, the Eastern sheet. The North York Moors National Park's information centres at Danby and Sutton Bank stock many waymarked walks leaflets as well as a large selection of other publications on the North York Moors.

The area is crossed by many long-distance paths, official and unofficial, such as the Cleveland Way, Wainwright's Coast to Coast Walk, the Lyke Wake Walk, the Derwent Way, the Crosses Walk, the White Rose Walk, the Bilsland Circuit, the Eskdale Way and the Esk Valley Walk, details of which can be obtained from the information centres. Early in 1994 the

National Park launched its link through the Tabular Hills Walk from Helmsley to Scarborough; this is waymarked with 'Link' signs, which you will see from time to time on walks on the southern side of the park.

If you enjoy walking and would like to make sure that the footpath network is preserved and enhanced, please consider supporting the Ramblers' Association, information on which can be obtained from the Ramblers' Association, 1/5 Wandsworth Road, London SW8 2XX.

As you walk, please remember the Country Code:

> Enjoy the countryside and respect its life and work.
> Guard against fire risks.
> Fasten all gates.
> Keep dogs under control.
> Keep to public paths across farm land.
> Use gates and stiles to cross fences, hedges and walls.
> Leave livestock, crops and machinery alone.
> Take your litter home.
> Help to keep all water clean.
> Protect wild life, plants and trees.
> Take special care on country roads.
> Make no unnecessary noise.

NORTH YORK MOORS NATIONAL PARK

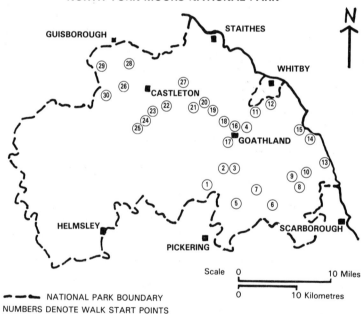

Area map showing locations of the walks.

6

NEWTON DALE, STONY MOOR
AND RAIN DALE

WALK 1

★

4 or 6½ miles (6.5 or 10.5 km)

Delightful valleys on good paths, moorland and forest, excellent views, and most within earshot if not within sight of the North Yorkshire Moors Railway. The walk starts from Levisham Station (GR 818 910), so is equally suitable for those arriving by train or by car. Levisham is sign-posted off the A169 Pickering to Whitby road about 5 miles north of Pickering. There are fine views from this minor road. Drive to the top end of Levisham, an attractive village with a large green, where the road to the station is signposted. Park in the station car park (fee).

Leave the car park and turn right over the cattle-grid and up the road towards Levisham. In 60 yards a public footpath sign points right over a sleeper bridge and through a gate into woodland. Follow the clear path up through the wood, which you leave by another gate. Bear very slightly right up the large field to a stile by a prominent gate at the top. A few yards to your right is a footpath sign with a fork in the track just beyond it: take the green track slanting uphill signposted 'Village'. Already there is a fine view over Newton Dale. A few yards before you reach a well-sited bench the track forks again: keep right on the lower path which passes in front of the bench and contours round with a steep drop to the right before bearing right and climbing to a stile. Now keep forward with a wall to your left through two fields. Levisham village appears ahead. Cross a stile by a gate and emerge onto a narrow tarmac lane.

The village is straight ahead, but your route turns right along the lane (Little Field Lane) for about 400 yards to where shortly after you pass a power line pole a bridleway sign points left down a rather overgrown fenced way. Soon the narrow path bears left and you have a steep wooded slope to your right. Look out for where the path forks right near a wooden fence with a blue arrow on it, drops to cross the head of a valley and climbs into the wood on the other side. Soon you reach the motor road you drove along earlier: turn right downhill, until a 'Link' sign points you right down a stony track. When the track forks three ways, the middle one going through a gate ahead, keep left downhill on a less clear track, which leads past the derelict St Mary's church and over a footbridge. Turn right for a few yards to a gate and keep straight ahead up the track.

When you come to a much better track (Sleights Road) turn right along it and follow this pleasant old way all the way down the valley of

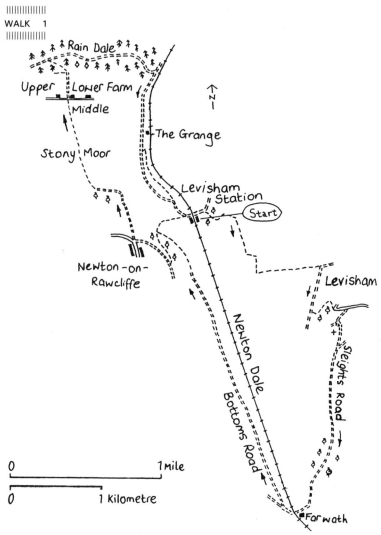

Levisham Beck, passing through several gates, until eventually you pass
through a gate and emerge from the trees into a field. At the bottom of
this field the track forks: keep right through a gate with the beck
immediately to your right. Pass to the right of the houses at Farwath,
cross the railway and the footbridge, and keep forward along the track.
Where it begins to climb, take a minor track forking right off it, and now
follows another delightful valley track, parallel to the railway but some
way from it, remote and peaceful.

8

Eventually the track passes through several fenced fields by gates and narrows to a footpath. Pass through another gate and enjoy a fine open view over Newton Dale to your outward route; Levisham Station appears half-right ahead. The path climbs to a gate: keep forward and upward. Pass through a large gate into a more open field and bear slightly left on the clear path uphill. Cross a stile by a gate and keep forward and up to a clear cross track. For the SHORTER WALK turn right on this down-hill, following an old hollow way to a clearer track with the station immediately below; bear right downhill, cross a footbridge and return to the starting point.

For the LONGER WALK turn left at the cross track uphill to a stile into the wood and follow the clear path up to a stony track at the top of which you turn right. Where the track bears left there is a superb view over Newton Dale. Follow the track to the village of Newton-on-Rawcliffe. If you want to have a look at the village keep forward to the tarmac road and turn left, but our walk turns right by the 'Link' signpost a yard or two before you reach the tarmac. The track soon begins to descend Newton Banks, and there are more glimpses of Newton Dale. At a fork go left or right — they soon meet up again — and follow the track until you pass through a gate, ford a beck, and bear left up a clear path through more open woodland with bilberries and heather. The clear path climbs gently over Stony Moor, at its best when the heather is in bloom.

Emerge at a cross track by a house (Middle Farm — Upper and Lower Farms can be seen to left and right); cross straight over the track, pass through the gate opposite, to the left of the house, and keep forward along the grassy track. Soon you must go through a wooden barrier (ignore the blue arrow pointing left here) and along a clear narrow path which soon descends through woodland into Rain Dale. Negotiate two more barriers and reach a forest road: turn right on it down the valley to a T-junction with a tarmac road, where again you turn right. This road will lead you back to the starting point, but there is a detour onto a footpath which you may prefer. About 200 yards past a house on the left called The Grange waymarks point left down some concrete steps and over a footbridge; on the far side of this ignore the yellow arrow pointing left and follow the red arrow on blue which points right. This clear path, with the beck to your right and the railway to your left, will also lead you back to Levisham Station.

(The last section of this walk, along the tarmac road, is part of a Forestry Commission Forest Drive: for a small toll you can drive through the forest past Raper's Farm picnic site and round to the public road north of Stape.)

HOLE OF HORCUM
AND LEVISHAM MOOR

WALK 2

★

5 miles (8 km)

This is a good clean dry moorland walk, most of the route of which can be seen when you stand on the edge of the Hole of Horcum at the starting point. Driving from Pickering on the A169 towards Whitby, about eight miles out of the town there is a large car park on the right-hand side (GR 852 937). Park here.

Cross the main road and walk forward a few yards to the edge of the drop, there turning right on a clear cross path on top of a low embankment. Follow this as far as the sharp bend on the main road, then keep forward along the track towards a gate, but 40 yards before the gate fork left (footpath sign) on a descending path to a ladder-stile. Cross this and follow the path which slopes on the side of the hill downhill to the bottom of the Hole. The track comes to a gate on the other side of a stream; go over the stile by the gate and follow the track as it passes to the right of the old house and walled enclosure of Low Horcum and down into a dip. A short way up the other side leave it to fork right on a clear path which passes midway between the wood on the left and the stream on the right.

The path eventually leads to a gate and stile into the woods, but ignore this and bear right along the outside of the boundary fence of the wood. Cross two stiles and follow the wall on your left, with the beck below to your right, as the path leads gently down to the level of the beck, which you cross by a footbridge. Bear left for a few yards as far as a small beck coming in from the right, cross this by a sleeper bridge and turn right up by the side of it (signposted Dundale Pond). From here to the top of the moor the stream is on the right, or rather the stream bed, because usually the water course is dry. The path is very clear and rises gently; ravines and old trees help to make a pleasant scene.

Shortly after the trees in the ravine on the right end the path forks: keep right up the shallow depression to a footpath sign which you will see in the distance. At the signpost you reach Dundale Pond, where a plaque informs you that this small valley was given to the monks of Malton Priory in about 1230 as pasture for their animals and that the pond was probably made at this time as a place for stock to drink. Take a right-angled turn to the right here onto a very clear track going over the moor. The route can soon be seen a long way ahead, indicated by occasional

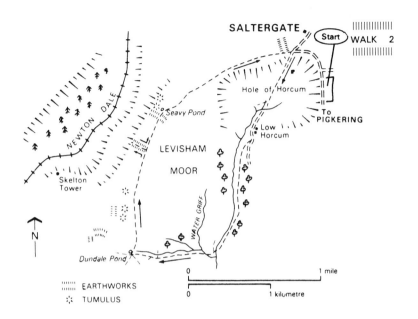

SALTERGATE

Start WALK 2

Hole of Horcum

To PIGKERING

Seavy Pond

Low Horcum

LEVISHAM

MOOR

NEWTON DALE

Skelton Tower

WATER GRIFF

N

Dundale Pond

0   1 mile

0   1 kilometre

⸽⸽⸽⸽⸽ EARTHWORKS

∴ TUMULUS

concrete posts. So far your way has been largely through bracken, but from now on it is through heather.

Ancient earthworks and tumuli abound in these parts. About 1,200 yards to the north of Dundale Pond look out for another plaque on a low stone to the left of the track, which marks an Iron Age dyke, a large ditch with two banks, probably constructed as a territorial boundary. At this point it is worth leaving the track along a clear path on the left which follows the line of the earthwork to the edge of the moor. Here is one of the most dramatic views of Newton Dale with its railway snaking along the steep-sided wooded valley. Halfway down on the left can be seen Skelton Tower. This viewpoint would be a fine spot for a picnic.

Now return to the track and resume your journey along it, passing another similar long earthwork on the left and the little Seavy Pond. The wide trail continues over the moor, eventually skirting the top of the Hole of Horcum, known by many as the Devil's Punchbowl. Legend has it that the devil, or perhaps a giant, scooped the soil and rock out of the moor to form the Hole of Horcum and dumped the debris a mile or so to the east to make Blakey Topping. The Romans are known to have used the Hole as an encampment. Shortly before you reach the road another plaque on a low stone to the left of the track provides information about Bronze Age barrows. Just before you reach the road, Saltergate Inn, taking its name from the fact that it was on the old salt route from Robin Hood's Bay, and the Fylingdales Early Warning Station can be seen to the left. Pass through the gate and return by your outward route to the car.

11

BLAKEY TOPPING
AND SALTERGATE BROW

WALK 3

★

4 miles (6.5 km)

This is a straightforward dry walk which includes a steep but short pull up to the summit of Blakey Topping, a fine sugar loaf outlier of the Tabular Hills which extend from Scarborough in the east to Black Hambleton in the west. The starting point is the same car park as for Walk 2.

Turn right out of the car park and walk past the AA telephone along the verge in the direction of Whitby. In about 200 yards turn right along a narrow tarmac road through the conifers ('Link' sign). Cross a stile by a gate with a notice indicating that this is a private road to Newgate Foot Farm. Soon Blakey Topping comes into view half-left in front. Just before a National Trust sign for the Bridestones bear left down the concrete track to the farm. Enter the farmyard and bear left with the concrete road, which continues downhill as a stony track. Keep straight forward past two old Nissen huts towards the Topping. Where the track bears right, go through the stile straight ahead and walk forward with the fence to your left, soon crossing another stile in it and bearing right on the clear path up to the summit.

Particularly noticeable in the view is the Fylingdales Early Warning Station and a sea of forest. Retrace your steps downhill and over the two stiles, but when you reach the track, instead of keeping downhill towards the farm turn right through a wooden kissing-gate into the forest and follow the path between the trees and the moor. Shortly after the path acquires trees on both sides you join a forest road and bear right along it. Where it forks almost immediately, keep left. Follow this road until you come to a wide ride through the trees on the left: looking along it you will see the old stone Malo Cross and a footpath signpost beyond it. Make for the cross, leaving the forest through a gate. The Malo Cross is one of the many crosses of ancient origin to be found on the moors.

Ignore a stile on the right and the path ascending the hill on the left and keep forward on the track with a fence to your right (the signpost points to Horcum). A steady but gentle rise alongside Whinny Nab takes you up to Saltergate Brow. Snaking across the moor is the Pickering to Whitby road, beyond which is the depression of Newton Dale. Rejoin the grasslands on reaching the top, the path conforming to the shape of Saltergate Brow. Saltergate Inn comes into view and you pass through a

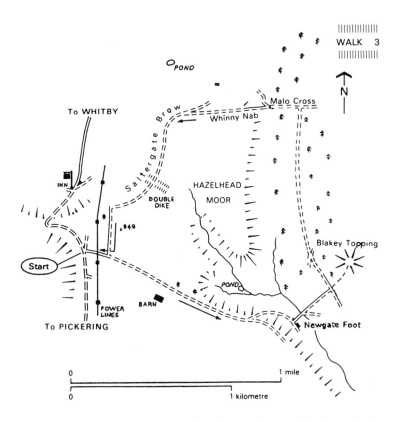

gate before heading for a conifer plantation and a row of pylons. At the trees go through the gate and immediately turn left between the fence and the wood. Soon you rejoin the narrow tarmac road and follow it to the right back to the main road and the car.

13

WHINSTONE RIDGE, ROBIN HOOD'S BAY ROAD AND LILLA HOWE

WALK 4

★

7½ miles (12 km)

For a good walk, full of interest all the way, this one takes a lot of beating. In dry conditions, the ability to step out at a good pace, sniffing the ozone from the sea and the scents from the moor (the walk is best in August, when the heather is in bloom), examining the points of interest on the way, makes the distance seem much less than it really is, especially bearing in mind that most of the walking is on level ground.

The narrow ridge of volcanic rock, extensively quarried for its hard grey stone used for road making, extends from the North York Moors, through Teesdale at High Force, to the Western Isles of Scotland. The long quarries show where the molten rock was forced through narrow fissures. We are to follow the course of the ridge as far as the Robin Hood's Bay Road at Blea Hill Beck. This ancient highway, now merely depressions in the heather moor, was once the route taken by traders in salt, and smugglers too, from Robin Hood's Bay to Saltergate, Pickering and beyond. We shall follow it as far as Lilla Howe, probably the oldest of all the ancient crosses on the moors, and pause for views of the Fylingdales Early Warning Station, part of the Derwent Valley, the forests and the coast beyond. The return will be on a good track past many old cairns.

Just south of the Goathland turning 6½ miles from Whitby on the Pickering road a public bridleway is signposted at a large layby on the east side of the road. Park here (GR 855 026). Cross the stile by the gate and walk along the bridleway. A short distance along are two standing stones with interesting inscriptions ('Sneaton (?) Liberty Assizes 1784'; 'at York Assizes 18 – – '). Just before you pass under power lines there is a quarry to the right of the track, and soon you have a forest fence to your left, although the trees are some way off. Pass through a gate, and now you are inside the fence. For a short distance only the forest comes close to the track. The track begins to climb gently and near the top of the slope it forks (cairn): keep left (you return along the right-hand branch). From the highest point there are fine views left to the coast and here you pass the York Cross, now only a stump. Ahead in the forest can be seen a line of quarries along the Whinstone Ridge on Pike Hill (bare of trees) and your path ascending by them.

Enter the forest and pass along a wide ride to reach a forest road, where

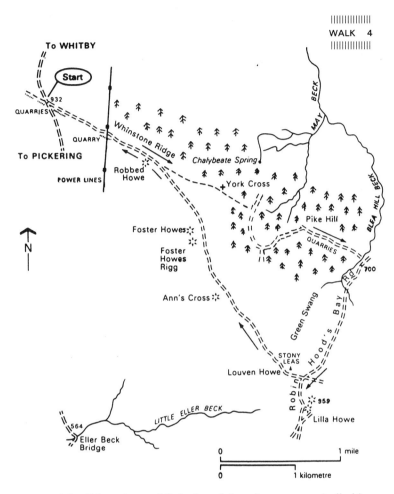

you turn right. When the road forks keep left and soon you are climbing past the quarries seen earlier. At a junction where there is a footpath signpost keep straight ahead uphill. At a fork in the track keep left and soon you reach another footpath signpost. Ignore this and keep forward on the track. Descend gently until you reach the forest fence, where you follow the track left for a few yards to a gate on the right. Pass through and bear right down the remaining slope to cross Blea Hill Beck; continue up the other side, soon reaching a hollow way, along which you bear right on a clear path. This is the Robin Hood's Bay Road, the route of which is never in doubt, for there are numerous marker cairns. As you climb look back for views to the coast.

Eventually you reach a clear crossroads with a signpost. The track

15

ahead leads to Saltergate and a short distance along it is Lilla Cross, where lies buried Lilla, one of the chief ministers of King Edwin of Northumbria, who in AD 626 saved his master's life by throwing himself between the king and the dagger of a would-be assassin. After visiting the cross and enjoying the views (including of course a close-up of the Fylingdales Station) return to this point and take the track signposted to Goathland.

Shortly after passing the trig point on Louven Howe you come to a broad cross-track: go right on this for a few yards before bearing left off it again on a narrower track through the heather (the forest fence is a short distance off to your right). You pass Ann's Cross, an upright stone on a tumulus, and then the twin tumuli of Foster Howes. From here the traffic on the main roads from Whitby to Pickering on the left and to Scarborough on the right can be seen, but it is sufficiently far away not to be disturbing. Here too you cross a stile by a gate and re-enter the fenced area of the forest. At a cairn you rejoin the Whinstone Ridge and your outward route, and there is a mile of walking to return to the car.

DALBY FOREST, CROSSCLIFF BROW
AND THE BRIDE STONES

WALK 5

★

4½ miles (7 km)

The Forestry Commission levy a toll of £2.50 for the privilege of driving through Dalby Forest, but it is money well spent, because as well as the 9-mile Dalby Forest Drive there are waymarked walks, picnic sites and an information centre and shop. I suggest you take a picnic and spend a day exploring this most attractive area of woodland. Our walk includes the Bride Stones, natural outcrops of hard-wearing siliceous sandstone and limestone which have stood up to the weather while the surrounding Corallian limestone has been worn away over the ages, leaving some striking rock shapes. This area is owned by the National Trust and is maintained by them, the Yorkshire Wildlife Trust and the Forestry Commission as a nature reserve.

Thornton Dale is one of Yorkshire's most famously beautiful villages and should not be missed; there is a large car park close to the village centre. Take the Whitby road out of Thornton Dale and after 1½ miles turn right along a minor road signposted Low Dalby: Forest Drive and follow it to the visitor centre and car park at Low Dalby, paying your toll on the way. After a look round the visitor centre, where leaflets about the waymarked walks and much else of interest can be obtained, continue by car along the Forest Drive for a further 3.2 miles, passing various picnic sites and car parks en route, until you reach the Staindale Lake car park, where you should leave the car in the park to the left of the road (GR 877 904).

Take the path leaving the back of the car park and cross the grass to the National Trust signpost visible at the far side. When you reach a kissing-gate and a gap-stile side by side go through the kissing-gate and follow the track. Just before the track fords a tree-lined beck bear right off it to another kissing-gate and National Trust sign. The path leads over the beck by a footbridge and up the side valley of Dove Dale. Soon you will see ahead of you the nab of Needle Point with a ribbon of path snaking up it. As you climb steeply up this well-made path you will see to your right over the valley of Bridestone Griff the Low Bride Stones, and as you reach the top of the slope the High Bride Stones are ahead of you.

When you reach the first of these stones you will notice a clear path to the right, heading back to the Low Bride Stones. Having explored the High Bride Stones, follow this path. It drops steeply to cross Bridestone

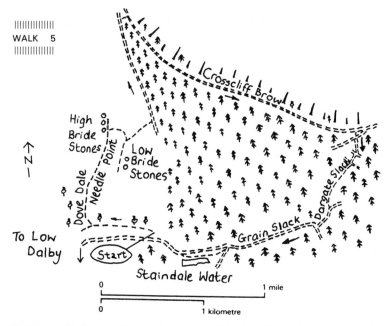

↑
N
|

High Bride Stones

Low Bride Stones

Needle Point

Dove Dale

Crosscliff Brow

Dargate Slack

Grain Slack

To Low Dalby ↓ Start

Staindale Water

0   1 mile

0   1 kilometre

Griff and climbs equally steeply up the other side. Near the top, 30 yards before you reach the first stone outcrop, fork left on a minor path through the bracken, which climbs steeply for a few yards to a cairn and a clear cross path. The Low Bride Stones lie to the right, but your way is to the left. There is a fine view back across the valley to the High Bride Stones. The clear path, which can be damp in places, heads towards the forest, and when you reach it turn left along its outside edge on a broad track.

About 200 yards before the fenced fields begin look out for a marker post on the right of the track with yellow arrows painted on it. At this point leave the track and go through the wood on a narrow path, crossing a stile on the way. Soon you reach a cross track, along which you turn right. You are now on the top of Crosscliff Brow, and as you walk there are many fine views to the left. You will notice Blakey Topping (Walk 3) and the Fylingdales Early Warning Station. Shortly after passing a forest road coming in from the right a bench on the left marks a viewpoint, and after you pass a ride on the right signposted 'Short Return Route to Car Park' there are two more benches with views. At a major fork the main route goes right (again marked as a return route to the car park), but keep left and soon reach the main Crosscliff Viewpoint, which has a superior bench and a view indicator.

Now you leave the track along the edge by taking the path going into the forest behind the viewpoint; the 'blue man' waymark shows that you are now on the route of the Forestry Commission's 16 mile Forest Walk (see also Walk 7). In a few yards cross over a broad forest road, still with the blue man. Where this well-made path makes a sharp turn left (to a car

18

park) keep straight ahead down a clear but unmade path (blue man waymark to the left). In a few yards cross straight over the next forest road (blue man) on a clear path. Where this forks keep left, and when you reach another forest road go left for a few yards then right off it (blue man) on a narrow path which descends the valley of Dargate Slack. You reach the next forest road at a broad open space, and here you leave the blue man, who goes left, and turn right to follow the track down Grain Slack.

Ignore a track forking right, and another forking back left just before a cottage, and reach the tarmac road on a bend. Go left for a few yards then fork right off the road on a grassy path to a large car park. From the far end of the car park take the tarmac path; it forks immediately; ignore the left-hand branch crossing a footbridge and keep right towards Staindale Water. There are two more forks, the left-hand branch leading in each case to a picnic table by the lake, surely two of the most pleasant sites for a picnic you will find. The path is parallel to the lake and soon rejoins the motor road, which you follow back to your starting point.

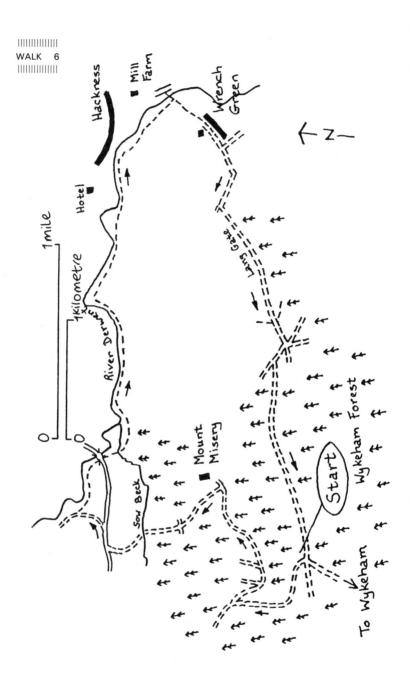

Hackness

Mill Farm

Wrench Green

N

Hotel

1 mile

1 kilometre

River Derwent

Lang Gate

Mount Misery

Sow Beck

Start

Wykeham Forest

To Wykeham

WYKEHAM FOREST
AND THE RIVER DERWENT

WALK 6

★

5 miles (8 km)

Woodland, a charming riverside path and superb views provide variety on this easy ramble.

In the hamlet of Wykeham on the A170 Pickering to Scarborough road take the minor road between the Downe Arms and the parish church, heading north. It soon enters Wykeham Forest, and when it reaches the edge of the escarpment of Highwood Brow there is a large parking place on the right. Park here (GR 942 889). There is a bench with a superb view north: to the left is Bickley Forest, ahead is Langdale Rigg (see Walk 7) with Lang Dale to the right of it (see Walk 9); a little further right is the hamlet of Broxa on top of the escarpment.

Follow the tarmac road descending steeply down the escarpment. When the gradient eases the tarmac ends; continue down the forest road, but take the first forest road forking off it on the right. Ignore two roads forking left off this one and follow it forward until you emerge from the forest with Mount Misery Farm ahead. Ignore the gateway leading to the farm and turn sharp left downhill. At a crossing of tracks keep forward through the gate; cross the bridge over Sow Beck and pass through another gate. The track leads up to a third gate and the motor road (there is a pleasant view left towards Troutsdale). Turn right along this, but only for 150 yards, when you fork half-left off it along a grassy track which soon leads to a gate. Shortly after this look out for a stile in the fence on the right (signposted), cross it and bear right, keeping close to the left-hand edge of the field, to descend to the river Derwent.

In the far left-hand corner of the field you join a track: follow the fence on your right, then continue along the river bank. When the fence bears right, bear slightly right across the middle of the field, slightly away from the river, cross the stile to the right of the bridge, and go straight over the road and over the stile opposite. Walk straight forward between bushes, then bear slightly right away from the bushes on the left, following the marker post, to recross Sow Beck by a sleeper bridge. Now bear left along the left-hand edge of the field with the beck to your left, soon reaching the point where it flows into the Derwent. Cross a stile and continue along the river bank. At one point care may be needed as at the time of writing some trees have collapsed into the river, taking the bank with them. The path is clear along the bank through woodland, with masses of bluebells in season.

A stile leads out of the wood, but the path continues by the river. Cross straight over the access track to Wood House Farm and the stile at the far side (ignoring of course the river bridge); cross another stile, then a ditch, then another stile in quick succession and bear left round the edge of the field, largely on the flood bank beside the river. Leave this field by a stile into woodland, climb to the top of the bank and bear left along the left-hand edge of the field. Pass to the right of a large metal gate and keep along the edge of the field. When the fence bears right at the far end, cross a stile straight ahead and bear right with a beck to your left and a deep pit to the right; but in a few yards you will find a stile on the left and a concrete bridge over the beck. Over this bear left round the edge of the field.

Soon you are back on the flood bank, at first with a large hotel on the other side of the river, then the houses of Hackness. Cross a stile and keep on along the river bank. Cross another stile and continue along the left-hand edge of the next field to the next stile. Now you are back on the flood bank. Cross the next stile — there is a footbridge over the river to your left — and now you leave the river by turning right up the field with the hedge to your right, towards the houses (no path). Cross the stile at the far end and walk forward to join the track through the hamlet of Wrench Green, and when you reach the tarmac keep forward up the steep and narrow Lang Gate. Ignore the entrance to Slack Farm on the right. There are fine views back as you climb, including a good view of Hackness Hall. The steep valley down to your right is Coomb Slack. At the top of the hill the tarmac ends and a broad forest road leads forward (ignore tracks left and right at this point) to a junction: turn right and follow this broad forest road back to the starting point.

LANGDALE RIGG AND FOREST

WALK 7

★

5 miles (8 km)

The Forestry Commission has provided the walker with access to country not allowed to the motorist. Walking in woodland has its own pleasures, even though viewpoints may be few and far between. In the early days blanket planting was practised, but now there is much more regard for the amenities. One route the Commission has pioneered for the benefit of the walker is the Forest Walk from Reasty Bank, above Harwood Dale, to Allerston on the Scarborough to Thornton Dale road, giving a day's walk of 16 miles, well marked with the sign of a man carrying a rucksack, blue on a white background. Today's route uses parts of this walk.

From all directions the car ride to the start is magnificent. The road north from Snainton goes through lovely Troutsdale; from Scarborough either through East Ayton and Forge Valley or through Scalby and Hackness. From all these points pass the Moorcock Inn at Langdale End and drive to the left of the isolated Howden Hill, taking the first fork to the right, signposted Birch Hall. If you approach the area from the Forest Drive through Bickley (see Walk 5) the fork is to the left just before reaching Howden Hill. Keep left at the next fork and continue until just before the woodland there is a layby on the left; or descend towards the bridge over Hipperley Beck and you will find another layby on the right just before the bridge. Park here (GR 928 924).

Retrace your steps along the road until you are almost back to Howden Hill. On the left there is a gateway with a public footpath sign. Go through and walk uphill by the hedge to the top of the field; keeping within the same field turn left and continue along the field edge to a gate on the right at the top. Go through and bear half-left (no path) up the slope, cross diagonally over a track and keep slanting up until you reach a clear grassy track on the left ascending through the bracken. Follow this. It quickly reaches the ridge of Langdale Rigg. Below on your right is the gorge of the river Derwent, a meltwater cut from the glacial age known as Lang Dale. Behind you is a delightful view of the valley of the Derwent as it makes its way towards another meltwater cut, the sylvan Forge Valley. Away on the left are the Bickley and Langdale Forests, beyond which is extensive moorland.

The track ascends the ridge. When it ends keep forward across the grass towards the forest, which you enter over a stile. Follow the grassy ride along until you emerge from the trees at the other end. At this point a

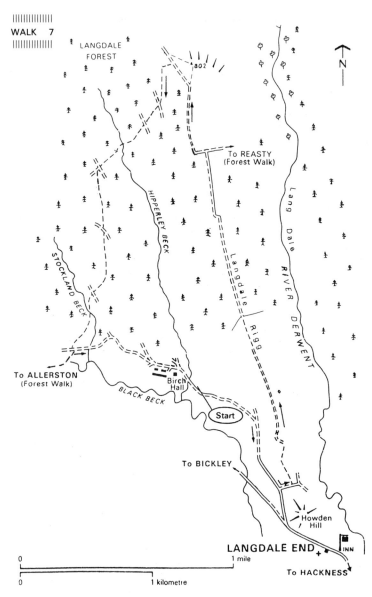

yellow arrow points straight ahead over barbed wire, but it is easier to turn left with the track. Here on the left is the first blue man waymark, showing that you have now joined the route of the Forest Walk, which you are going to follow for a good part of your walk. Soon the track bears right again and keeps along the top edge of the forest.

There is no right of way to the trig point on Langdale Rigg End, 802 feet above sea level, but it has considerable merit as a viewpoint. To visit it cross the fence on the right just before your track begins to descend, walk forward a yard or two, go through the gate on the left and follow a narrow path along near the left-hand edge of the slope, cutting right to the trig point when you draw level with it. The valley in front is that of the Derwent in its early stages. Near its source on the left is Lilla Rigg. The moors in front of you are Lownorth Moor, Harwood Dale Moor and on the horizon Fylingdales Moor (see Walk 10). To the north-east on a clear day should be a sight of the old windmill near Ravenscar. Thus can be seen, from Lilla Howe along the horizon to the windmill, the last weary eight miles of the Lyke Wake Walk. From the trig point return to the edge of the slope and bear right on a path slanting steeply downhill. Near the bottom cross over a cross path and make your way to a gate ahead. Go through and walk forward to rejoin the forest road. Turn left up it for about 100 yards until you find a blue man waymark pointing along a narrow path on the right into the forest.

If you do not make the detour to the trig point continue on the descending track until about 100 yards before the forest ends a blue man waymark points left along a narrow path through the trees. Now all you have to do is follow the blue man signs. The clear path leads to a forest road, which you cross straight over; parts of the next section can be wet. Cross straight over another forest road, cross Hipperley Beck by a footbridge and reach the next forest road at a junction; bear slightly left over this to find the continuation of the footpath. Soon fallen trees might make a slight detour necessary: the path keeps to the right of these, passes over a grassy ride and keeps forward uphill through bracken; this section is not so clear and you must follow the route trodden out closely. Soon however the path bears left and rejoins the much clearer original route.

Continue uphill. There is tall bracken to be negotiated — beware of obstacles on the ground hidden by it and pay attention to following the path. Cross straight over the next forest road; soon the path begins to drop and for a time you have a cleared area to the left. Cross another forest road; at all these crossings the continuation of the path is waymarked. The next stream, Stockland Beck, has to be forded. Soon you reach a track along which bear left and in 150 yards you meet a metalled forest road. Turn left along it, and as this is where we leave the waymarked Forest Walk ignore the continuation of the path which leaves this road on the right in a few yards. Bear right at the next junction of forest roads, and ignoring all further forks to left or right follow this road back to the car.

WHISPER DALES, LOW DALES, HACKNESS AND BEACON BROW

WALK 8

★

7½ miles (12 km)

The lovely valleys of Whisper Dales and Low Dales (always referred to in the plural, probably because of their multiple heads) are quiet retreats amid the surrounding forests. The trees, usually above the 400 foot contour, add something to the shapes of the hills enclosing the green pastures and rippling streams. Today we shall take a sample. We also include the charming hamlet of Hackness, a wild and romantic gorge and a woodland walk along the edge of an escarpment.

To reach the starting point, which is the car park at the top of Reasty Bank at the north-western end of the straight road on Suffield Moor (GR 964 944), from Scarborough turn left in Scalby and from Whitby turn right off the Scarborough road at the Harwood Dale sign, but at the next junction bear right, climbing the bank sloping up to the trees at the top. There is a large car park on both sides of the road. This is also the start of the Forestry Commission's 16-mile Forest Walk to Allerston.

After enjoying the extensive views of the coast and Harwood Dale below, cross to the west side of the motor road and enter the forest on a good forest road at right angles to the track along the cliff edge on your right. After 250 yards ignore a forest road forking right through a barrier with a notice saying 'No Vehicles Please' and keep forward, ignoring all tracks branching left or right, until the track descends out of the forest and Whisperdales Farm appears ahead. When the track forks, the right-hand branch going through a gate into the farm, keep left parallel to the beck on your left. After some time the track crosses the beck. Follow it over several stiles to the next farm, Lowdales.

At the farm cross the footbridge and stile, bear left with the track, cross another footbridge and leave the farm through a gateway. In a few yards, opposite a minor road on the right, fork half-left off the track to a stile by a gate and cross the next field parallel to the fence on your right to pass through a gap in the hedge ahead. Still walking parallel to the fence/hedge on the right make for a stile in the far right-hand corner of this field and cross the footbridge over Lowdales Beck (depending on the season, the reason for this field path may be immediately clear: the section of road between here and Lowdales Farm can also be the bed of Lowdales Beck!) Bear left along the lane with Lowdales Beck to the left and follow it down to the T-junction at Hackness.

26

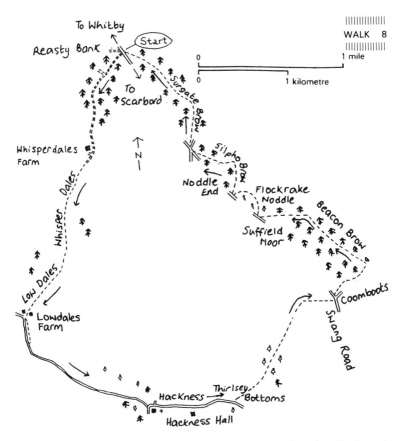

Turn left over the road bridge over Lowdales Beck and walk through the hamlet of Hackness. Ignore a minor road left to Silpho and consider a visit to the church of St Peter: there was a nunnery here from the late 7th century, and the church contains an Anglo-Saxon chancel arch and some fine sculpture and monuments. Shortly over the wall on the right can be seen the imposing late 18th century Hackness Hall. Pass under an ornamental footbridge and continue along the road, passing the entrance to the Hall on the right. Pass a signposted bridleway by a gate on the left, then a footpath on the right, and when you reach a signposted footpath on each side of the road, fork left off the road, ford Crossdales Beck and bearing slightly right follow the track up the valley of Thirlsey Bottoms. When the track begins to curve left you must bear half-right off it across the valley bottom towards the high bank and wood, and bear left along the bottom of this bank to reach a stile into the woods.

Keep forward up the valley on a faint path, which soon drops left into the valley bottom. Now make your way up the bottom of this narrow and

27

wild gorge, negotiating a number of fallen trees en route, to the far end, where a flight of old steps on the left leads you out of the wood and up to a footpath signpost. Follow the direction of Coomboots, in other words straight ahead through a gap in the hedge and on along the right-hand edge of the next field, with the continuation of the gorge down on your right. After this shallow valley ends, keep on along the fence/wall on the right until at a point where the fence bears right you reach a stile in it: cross, and walk along now with the fence to your left to another stile near the next corner. Keep forward through the trees to join a track, and bear left along it to the Swang Road.

Now you are going to follow four sections of path which swing in semicircles round the edge of an escarpment, in each case returning you to this road. So turn left along the road, ignoring the right fork to Burniston, but a few yards further on bear right along a signposted track into the woods. It leads eventually to the trig point on Beacon Brow, where the fine view is unfortunately restricted by the trees. The trig point is slightly to the right of the track, and after visiting it return to the track and continue along the edge of the escarpment. In places the track narrows to a footpath. Ignore a path forking left, and further on a track forking left through the trees, and you will reach a spot where the trees thin and there is a somewhat better view. After walking along a stretch where the way is a narrow footpath you reach another fork: the main path goes straight on, but you must bear left slightly uphill, soon to rejoin the road.

Turn right; a short distance along ignore a bridleway sign on the right, but 30 yards after that fork right off the road onto a clear path which bears right for a yard or two and then left on a clear path along a grassy ride in the forest. This path leads in a semicircle round the edge of Flockrake Noddle, and when you reach a fork where neither path is particularly clear, keep left to regain the road in a few yards. Turn right along the path beside the road and very soon you will reach a clear broad track going right into the wood (bridleway sign). Follow this track for a short distance to a junction, where you must fork left along another clear track. Now your way is round the edge of Silpho Brow, and again in time the path leads you back to the road. Turn right, to reach in a few yards a minor road on the right; go down this for 3 yards, then fork left off it on a clear path back into the wood. In a few yards keep right at a fork. Now your way lies round Surgate Brow on a path which is waymarked and which usually keeps fairly close to the edge, although the view is blocked by trees. Ignore at one point a track forking left, and your path/track will lead you back to the starting point on Reasty Bank.

HIGH DALES, LANG DALE
AND REASTY BANK

WALK 9

★

7½ miles (12 km)

A pleasant mixture of forest and valley walking, with some fine views. The starting point is the large car park on the top of Reasty Bank, as in Walk 8.

As in that walk, from the car park on the west side of the motor road enter the forest on a good forest road at right angles to the track along the cliff edge on your right. This time instead of ignoring the forest road forking right after 250 yards through a barrier with a notice saying 'No Vehicles Please', turn along it. When you reach a fork, keep left, and at the next T-junction again go left. About 40 yards further on there is another fork, at which you keep right, i.e. straight on. At the next major fork keep left, again straight ahead. Soon through the trees to your left you can see the valley of Ash Haggs Gill.

Now you must keep a careful look out for a blue arrow on a tree to the right of the track, pointing you right along a forest ride, and on the next section occasional blue paint marks on trees will confirm that you are on the correct route. After about 90 yards the clear path bears left (there is a blue mark on the tree on the left) and shortly you must ignore a ride forking left and another forking right and keep forward, soon on a narrow path dropping gently down a hollow way. Soon there is a brief glimpse right to the valley of High Dales with its farm, before the path continues its descent between high banks. Cross straight over a track and keep on down the hollow way. Soon Highdales Farm can be seen more clearly. Pass through a gate, and the clear path leads you down to another gate and a track just before Newgate House.

Turn left along the track, passing to the right of the house, through another gate and on along the access road, following the valley of Highdales Beck. On approaching Lowdales Farm the road crosses a track and 100 yards further on you reach a T-junction with the farmhouse just to your left. A raised footway and bridge on the left carry you dryshod over Lowdales Beck, which here flows cheerfully down the farm access road! Turn right along the road for a few yards, then fork half-left to a stile by a gate into a field. Walk forward to pass through a gateway in the facing hedge, then continue along the field parallel to the fence/hedge on your right to a stile and footbridge in the far right-hand corner. Having recrossed Lowdales Beck, which here leaves the road, turn right for a few

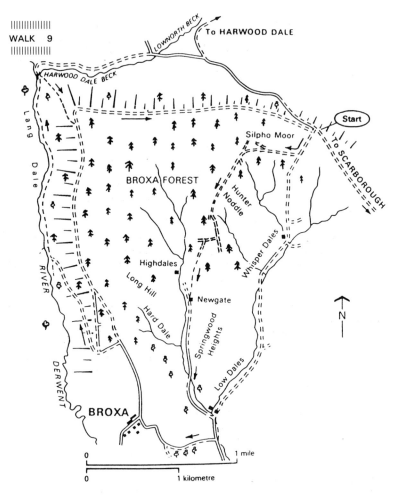

yards to find a track on the left by a sign saying 'No vehicle access'.

Soon you are in a gently ascending deep hollow way, and when it ends a clear path leads forward through the woods, a delightful stretch. The path leads to a track at the hamlet of Broxa. Turn right to pass Broxa Farm, and at the next junction, with the houses along to your left (and a fine view over the wall ahead towards Blakey Topping), bear slightly right along the narrow tarmac lane. When you reach the forest, fork left through a barrier and along the edge of the trees. On approaching the edge of the escarpment, ignore a forest road forking right and keep forward to the edge for a glorious view. At your feet is Lang Dale with the river Derwent, on the other side of the valley is Langdale Rigg (see Walk 7) and further left is Bickley Forest.

Take the descending track on your right, in a few yards crossing over a cross track. Eventually the track levels off, and a few yards after another track joins you from the left, your track forks. Take the left branch, again descending, and follow it all the way down to the valley bottom, where you bear right along the path by the Derwent. Sadly at present this lovely valley path attracts illegal motorcyclists and can be a river of mud: if this is still the case when you take your walk and it makes you as angry as it does me, please write and complain to the National Park Authority. Follow this path for over a mile, until you reach a metal footbridge over the river.

Ignore this and continue on the path, which in a few yards bears right uphill. There is a bench near the top of this steep ascent: ignore a path forking right at this point and keep on uphill with the steep drop to your left, but a short distance further on you do bear right for another stiff pull up. When you reach another track at a T-junction on a bend, keep straight on up it. It soon narrows, with the steep drop to Lang Dale on your right, and leads to a broad level forest road where you turn left. Soon there is another fine view left over Lang Dale to Langdale Rigg End and Langdale Forest beyond. The good track keeps close to the edge of the escarpment, and in time you reach a barrier and a broad forest road. A bench on the left here gives an excellent view over Harwood Dale to the route of Walk 10 and Harwood Dale Forest. Follow the forest road along the edge of Reasty Bank back to the car.

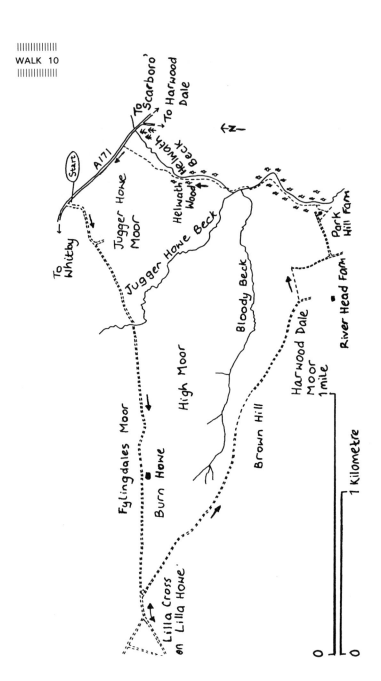

To Scarboro'

To Harwood Dale

A171

Start

To Whitby

Jugger Howe Moor

Jugger Howe Beck

Helwath Beck

Helwath Wood

Bloody Beck

High Moor

Fylingdales Moor

Burn Howe

Brown Hill

Harwood Dale Moor

Park Hill Farm

River Head Farm

Lilla Cross on Lilla Howe

N

0   0
1 mile
1 Kilometre

JUGGER HOWE MOOR, LILLA CROSS AND HELWATH

WALK 10

★

10 miles (16 km)

A splendid moorland leg-stretcher, at first on the route of the Lyke Wake Walk, with extensive views, is followed by a delightful, remote, peaceful woodland path by a gurgling beck. The tracks and paths are clear for almost the whole route, but the last section passes through dense bracken in summer.

About 10 miles north of Scarborough on the A171 to Whitby, shortly after a minor road forking left signposted 'Harwood Dale 3', a loop of the old road forms a large layby on the right. Ignore this and continue in the Whitby direction for a short distance until another loop of the old road forms another very large layby, this time on the left; access to it is by a break in the heather bank on the left and along a concrete track. Park in the layby (GR 945 002).

The concrete track leads through a gate; cross the stile and follow the track over the moor, a blaze of colour in August when the heather is in bloom. There are distant views in all directions. Where the concrete road makes a sharp turn left, keep straight on along the grassy track, which eventually becomes narrower and stonier and drops very steeply into the cross valley of Jugger Howe Beck. Pass over the footbridge and climb steeply up the other side. Follow the track past the large cairn on Burn Howe and keep on it until another very clear track comes in from the left (from the direction of Scarborough and the sea in the distance). This will be your return route, but first you keep forward, soon seeing Lilla Cross prominent on the skyline. At the next fork keep left for the cross. After visiting it return to the clear fork, which has a large boulder between the arms, and bear right for the return route.

Follow this track all the way down to where it ends as the fenced fields begin. Pass through the gate and keep along the fence on your left; at first there is no clear path, but soon a very stony track is reached, which leads through another gate onto a much better track. Follow this track until you reach a footpath signpost on the left. Go through the gate, following the direction to Chapel Farm, and walk down the field with the fence to your left. The next section of the path is well waymarked with blue arrows. Go through a gate and keep on by the fence, but only until you reach a gate in it. Here turn sharp right on a clear track across the field, soon with a fence to your right. Pass through the gate at the end of the

33

field and turn left down the track, ignoring the track straight ahead.

About 50 yards before Park Hill Farm leave the track through a gate on the right (waymark) and follow the fence on your left down to a gate in it; go through and walk forward a few yards to a footpath sign, where you bear right down to a stile into the wood. The path down through the wood is clear, but quite steep, and you meet a cross path at the bottom. Turn left along it. The beck is a few yards off to the right. There follows a lovely stretch of woodland walking; the path is always clear, but can be overgrown and the bracken high in summer. Eventually you reach a stile by a gate, and a few yards further cross the beck by a footbridge on the right.

Turn immediately left, now with the beck to your left. Keep always to the path which is closest to the beck, but do not ford a side beck coming in from the right: bear right at this point and keep this beck to your left, but in a short distance you cross it by a footbridge and bear right along a clear path. Watch out for a fork where you bear left on a clear ascending path through the bracken. Near the top you emerge from the bracken onto heather moorland and the path leads to a stile in a fence. Cross this and keep forward (no path) with a fence to your left, bearing right with it at the far end of the field and then in a few yards half-left again to a stile by a gate. Keep forward on a faint track with a line of old trees to the right.

Soon the track becomes very clear. It first bears slightly right, then curves left and descends to cross a beck, then rises again, passes to the right of a ruined building and bears slightly left to a gate. Follow the track to the main road (public footpath sign) and turn left to return to the car.

LITTLEBECK AND FALLING FOSS

WALK 11

★

4 miles (6 km)

The deep valley of Little Beck with its delightful tiny hamlet of Littlebeck and the fine waterfall of Falling Foss, some 50 feet high, is a must for walkers. Falling Foss is signposted from the B1416 Ruswarp to Scarborough road about 1½ miles from where this joins the A171 Whitby to Scarborough road. Follow the minor road down to find the Forestry Commission Falling Foss car park and picnic site on the left. Park here (GR 888 035). A notice board gives details of a number of waymarked walks in the surrounding Sneaton Forest. Perhaps our short ramble will serve as an appetizer.

Return to the access road and turn left downhill (signposted Falling Foss). Ignore paths leaving it on the right and follow it down to cross May Beck, one of the feeders of Little Beck, by a stone bridge. A few yards further on turn left on the path with a signpost which indicates that you are now on A.Wainwright's Coast to Coast route. The track descends and you cross the beck by stepping-stones. When you reach a T-junction (red marker) bear right downhill and at the next fork bear right to cross a footbridge. Follow the main path forward, soon with May Beck again to your right. Eventually the path leads up by steps to a stile: keep forward on the clear path, which soon drops again to the beck side. Keeping the beck on your right, you will soon see the May Beck car park on the other side.

Follow the path to the road and turn right over the bridge. Leaving the car park on your right continue up the forest road, still with May Beck down to your left, past a notice forbidding unauthorised vehicles. Ignore a footpath sign pointing left off the road, but 100 yards further on cross a signposted stile on the right, bear right for 30 yards, then left on a grassy track towards the wood, which you enter by a stile. Ignore a second stile beyond it on the right and keep forward. The path follows the top edge of the wood. Ignore two stiles in the fence on the left and a path branching off right. The path begins to drop away from the edge of the wood and you reach a fork, where you bear left on the less clear path which soon follows a grassy ride. As you approach the end of the wood the path bears left and soon you reach a track.

Bear right along the track, but immediately fork left (bridleway sign) to pass to the left of Foss Farm and through another gate. Soon a recessed gateway is seen on the right (bridleway sign); go through it onto a cart

35

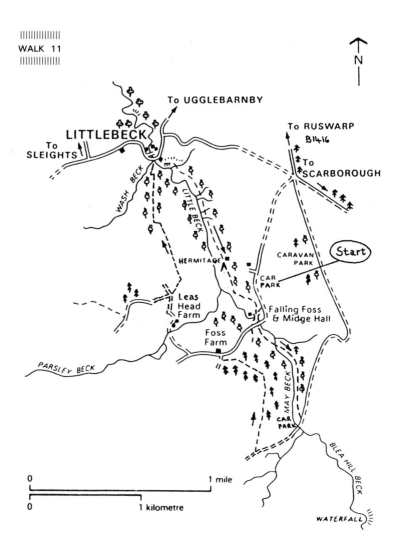

road, partly sunken, on the left-hand side of a field. Pass through a gate (with a notice saying Leashead), cross Parsley Beck, another feeder of Little Beck, and follow the track towards the farm. Immediately before you reach it, turn left on the waymarked path to a stile and walk forward to reach the farm access road, on which you bear left. It leads to a gate, where another track comes in from the left. You will see two gates on the right: go through the second of these (bridleway sign) and keep down the right-hand edge of the field on a grassy track. Pass through another gate and immediately bear left, now with a hedge to your left, at first on a narrower footpath, but after passing (and ignoring) two adjacent gates in this hedge the track becomes clear again.

Pass through another gate and the track bears left to another gate into the wood (bridleway sign). Keep along the top edge of the narrow wood, now with the hedge to your right again. After passing through another gate a sign informs you that you have entered the Yorkshire Wildlife Trust's Little Beck Wood Nature Reserve. Keep forward on the narrow footpath, which soon enters the wood proper and descends to the hamlet of Littlebeck. Either bear right along the road to cross the ford, or if this is under water walk forward along the road, soon branching right off it along a path which leads to a footbridge. Follow the road uphill to a bench behind which is a kissing-gate with a notice on it to Falling Foss.

This lovely woodland path has no difficulties of route-finding. At one point where there is a cave straight ahead look out for a signpost pointing you right up a flight of steps. In time the path leads you high above the valley floor, close to the top edge of the wood, and here you will reach the 'Hermitage', an enormous hollowed out rock; above the fine doorway is carved 'G.C. 1790'. It is said that this was the cell of a monk from Whitby who left the abbey in search of greater peace. Now keep forward along the upper path, but in just over 100 yards you must fork right, and for a short distance you have a wall on your left. When you reach a 'C to C' (i.e. Coast to Coast) signpost pointing through an old gateway in a wall on the right, follow it, and soon you will hear the sound of Falling Foss, well seen from the railing a short distance before the house known as Midge Hall. Standing facing the waterfall, look over your right shoulder and you will see a partly paved but badly eroded path climbing steeply to a bridleway sign at the top. Follow this up to the road and bear left to return to the car.

SLEIGHTS, SNEATON
AND THE MONK'S WALK

WALK 12

★

8 miles (12.5 km)

A ramble in the attractive undulating country south-west of Whitby, including a fine section of paved path, pleasant woodland paths and fine views. Park in the village of Sleights, just off the A169 Pickering to Whitby road and just south of the bridge over the river Esk, in a free car park near the Salmon Leap Hotel (GR 867 081).

Leave the car park and turn left down the road past the hotel towards the station. Just before the level crossing turn right up Lowdale Lane, then left across the bridge over Iburndale Beck along Echo Hill. Immediately after passing a football pitch on the right, go left at the T-junction. The track climbs, then drops again: ignore a gateway straight ahead and turn right up the track behind a row of houses. Pass through a gate ahead and continue up the grassy track, passing through another gate with a footpath signpost. To your left is the Esk valley. The track is close to the right-hand edge of the field, and Whitby Abbey is visible left as you climb. Just before a cross hedge turn left at the signpost, keeping this hedge to your right. At the next cross hedge kink right and then left (signposts), then continue the direction as before, soon with a hedge now to your left. Cross a stile and keep forward, bearing right twice round the edge of the field, to turn left through a gateway in the top corner. Now follow the fence on your left, parallel to the Esk valley, cross a stile in the next corner and keep forward on the grassy path, dropping to cross the shallow valley ahead.

Bear slightly right up the track to a stile by a gate, then up across the middle of the next field, turning left at the far side over the stile by the signpost. The track passes to the left of all the buildings of Hagg House and soon drops to a stile by a gate. Descend towards the Esk valley, a few yards from the right-hand edge of the field, to a stile by a gate with a house ahead. Bear left to a gate and cross the Esk Valley railway. Through the gate on the other side bear right along the track. The spire of Ruswarp church is soon visible ahead, and as you pass through the next gate you are close to the Esk. Pass to the right of a white house, through a kissing-gate, recross the railway, through another kissing-gate and continue up the stony track, soon bearing right at a fork over a cattle-grid.

In a few yards, where the track bears right, keep straight on (footpath

38

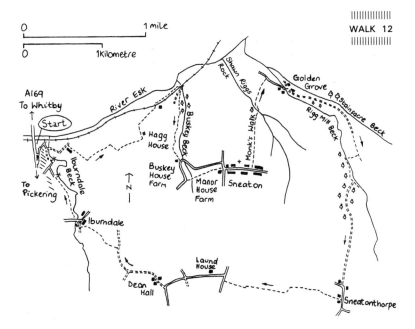

sign) on a clear path leading towards the wood. Follow the right-hand edge of the wood, soon climbing quite steeply to a stile. Follow the left-hand edge of the next field to a stile by a gate and signpost, then keep your direction, parallel to the fence to your right. Pass through a gap in a hedge and keep forward along a reasonably clear path up the middle of the next field to another stile. Now follow the hedge on your right, pass through another gap in a hedge and keep along the right-hand edge of the field to the next stile by a gate. Walk forward towards Buskey House Farm, pass through a gate and to the left of the farmhouse and out on to the motor road.

Keep forward along the road, but where it curves sharply right cross the signposted ladder-stile on the left and cross the end of the narrow field to the next stile. Drop steeply to the next stile, cross Buskey Beck by the footbridge and bear left on a paved path up through the wood. Steps lead up to a stile out of the wood. Keep forward up the middle of the next large field, with a fine view to Whitby and the sea, to a stile by a gate, then across the middle of the next field to a stile in the facing fence, from which the next stile can be seen ahead. Pass to the left of Manor House Farm to another stile and the road at a junction in Sneaton. Keep forward along Beacon Way (a no through road) past Sneaton Hall Hotel.

Look out for a track on the left through the yard of Monk's Farm, signposted Footpath to Whitby, which leads to a hedged paved path. This is the lovely old Monk's Walk. After a time there is the wooded ravine of Shawn Riggs Beck to your left, and the path curves down to cross the

39

beck by a footbridge, then leads beside the beck to another footbridge, after which the paving is intermittent. Soon you are in a broad hedged way, with Ruswarp to your left over the valley. When you reach a tarmac lane turn right along it and follow it to the houses of Golden Grove, where you cross Rigg Mill Beck and keep forward along the road marked Unsuitable for Motors. The road soon begins to climb through woodland and shortly you are walking along a fairly level ridge with a wooded valley on each side. The tarmac ends by a bungalow and you enter Cock Mill Wood. Ignore a clear path forking left, then a signposted footpath both left and right, and go through a gate ahead along a fenced way.

Pass through another gate and keep forward close to the right-hand edge of the field with a wooded ravine to your left. When you reach a clear track, with a metal gate ahead, turn right down a few yards of hedged way to find a small gate in the left-hand corner, leading to a clear narrow path, which drops to re-cross Rigg Mill Beck by a footbridge. Climb steeply up the bank and turn left along the clear cross path through Rigg Mill Wood. At one point you cross a side beck, with a little waterfall, by a plank bridge. As you approach the end of the woods, by various small wooden buildings, you reach a track: turn right up this, and follow it at first through the woods, then along the edge of them and finally through fields, until you reach the next motor road, where you turn left through Sneatonthorpe.

The road curves right and descends. Pass the entrance into Russell Hall, and you will reach a footpath sign on the left of the road pointing right up a concrete track to the right of a barn. Walk up through the yard to a gate, then on up the fenced way into the field and forward with the hedge to your right to two stiles close together, then on with the fence/hedge to your right to a stile and footbridge at the far end of this field. Now bear very slightly left (there is a signpost) up the middle of the next very large field, and in a few yards you will see another signpost in the hedge at the top. Cross the stile and keep your direction up the middle of the next field to the next signpost. When you reach the hedge turn left along the near side of it for 60 yards, then go through a gateway in it, bear left to another gateway into the next field, then bear right and follow the fence on your right.

There is a fine view right to Whitby and the sea. Cross the stile in the far right-hand corner of the field, then the ditch by a sleeper bridge, then another stile, then bear right along the right-hand edge of the next field. In the far corner of this field bear left for a few yards to find the next stile and another sleeper bridge, then keep the hedge to your right to the next stile. Walk through the narrow belt of trees, over a stone step-stile in a facing wall, to another wooden stile and the B1416 Ruswarp to Scarborough road. Turn right, but take the next road on the left signposted to Littlebeck and Sleights. At the next junction ignore the road right to Sleights and keep forward. Soon a fine view opens up right to Eskdale and Sleights, straight ahead to Littlebeck.

Immediately after the road curves left fork sharply right off it down a lane signposted to Dean Hall. Bear right with the road between the houses at Dean Hall, then left downhill. When the tarmac ends keep forward along the track. At the next fork, with a gate between the two branches, keep right, and soon the track narrows to a hedged footpath with intermittent paving. Look out for a waymarked stile on the left, cross it and walk straight down the field to a stile just to the right of a gateway in the hedge. Now bear very slightly right downhill to cross a dip in the ground to the next stile in the hedge below. Bear right with the hedge to your right to a stile by the large metal gate. Now head half-left down the next field to a stile by a gate in the bottom corner. Bear half-left again to another stile to the right of another metal gate (the furthest left of the several gates you can see ahead), which leads into a narrow fenced path.

Cross the stile at the bottom, go through the gate on the right and follow the track through the charming hamlet of Iburndale, forking left in it to the motor road, and there bearing left over Iburndale Beck. Take the first track on the right, going left in a few yards up a signposted ginnel, then right along a fenced path. Soon you are beside the beck, but not for long. You are led into another narrow fenced path. Pass through a metal kissing-gate; for a short time you are close to the beck again; pass through another kissing-gate, and you reach a tarmac road by a footbridge on the right. Ignore this and keep forward, bearing right at the next fork, then at the foot of the road ignore another footbridge ahead and turn left along the private road which is a public bridleway. Pass through a gateway and a road comes in from the right over a bridge. Now you are back on your outward route. Just before you reach the level crossing turn left to return to the car.

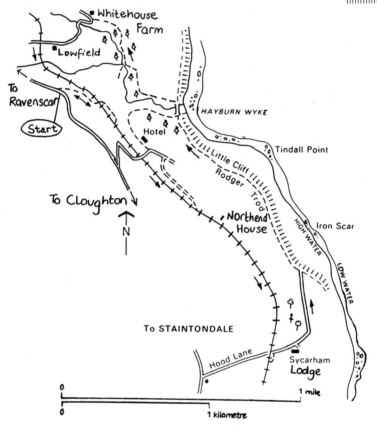

HAYBURN WYKE

WALK 13

★

4 miles (6.5 km)

A wooded glen running down to the sea, Hayburn Wyke is a beauty spot which was particularly popular when the railway was running between Scarborough and Whitby, providing a scenic ride second only in grandeur to the Pickering/Whitby line. It is now a nature reserve owned by the National Trust. The Cleveland Way passes through it.

Leave the A171 Scarborough to Whitby road in Cloughton, taking the minor road signposted to Ravenscar. Shortly after passing the entrance to the Hayburnwyke Hotel on the right the road descends a 1 in 7 hill, at the foot of which there is a long narrow layby on the left with a public footpath sign opposite on the right. Park here (GR 000 971).

The footpath sign points over a stile by a gate. Follow the track through the field; it soon bears right and becomes a grassy way between trees. Cross another stile by a gate, and a stone bridge over the old railway track on the right gives access to this track, now a permissive footpath. Turn left along it. After passing a red-brick house on the right and glimpsing the hotel through the trees on the left you cross the hotel access road and continue along the railway track.

Pass the attractive whitewashed and red-pantiled Northend House. Shortly after the view opens up again, to Scarborough and the sea, you cross a stone bridge over a minor road and immediately go through a gap in the fence on the left to descend and join this tarmac lane. Turn right along it. Where the tarmac ends at the restored Sycarham Lodge bear left up a stony track. From a bench halfway up take a breather to admire Cloughton Wyke, a stony cove immediately below, and Scarborough in the middle distance. Pass a public footpath sign and follow the track until you join the Cleveland Way on the cliff edge. Turn left along it. The cliffs hereabouts are magnificent and the path is along the edge, going gradually uphill, soon to be protected by thorn bushes.

This lovely section of coast path leads to a stile and a steep drop into the wooded Hayburn Wyke. Where the path forks it is worth going left for a few yards to a National Trust information board about the nature reserve, but the walk continues down the steps along the Cleveland Way. Almost at the cliff edge you must bear left at a fork to reach in a few yards a bench and viewpoint, then continue down the clear path with the wooded valley on your right; the descent is steep, there are steps, and you reach a broad cross path with the noise of waterfalls in the valley in front.

43

Turn right downhill, again partly by steps, to reach a fork: go right if you want to visit the beach, but the walk goes left down some more steps to a footbridge.

More steps lead steeply up the other side. Just after a National Trust sign on the right we leave the Cleveland Way by crossing a stile on the left signposted Staintondale. The clear path continues to climb, with the steep valley down to the left, and soon leads along the top edge of some open ground. Just before the far end of this look out for a clear path forking left and descending. Pass a redundant stile and continue with a steep drop to your left. Descend gently to stream level, where the path forks: ignore the left-hand branch which crosses a footbridge and bear right up the valley. Watch out for one point where the path bears left down steps to stream level. The path stays by the beck for some time before climbing again to reach a farm access road. Turn left along this.

You reach a minor road at Whitehouse Farm and bear left down it. Shortly after passing Lowfield campsite you reach a bridge over the old railway track. Cross the stile in the fence on the right immediately before it, drop down the steps and turn left along the track. When you reach the next high bridge across the old railway you want to be on the track which leads over it but there is no access at this point. So keep on along the railway until you reach the broad gateway on the left which you came through earlier. Go through and bear left along the edge of the field, taking care not to miss the start of the path forking left before the end of the field. Cross over the old railway bridge and follow the track back to the car.

RAVENSCAR AND STOUPE BROW

★

4½ miles (7 km)
A visit to Stoupe Beck Sands would add threequarters of a mile
or one kilometre to the round trip.

This is a simple walk combining moorland heather with glorious coastal
views. On the outward journey Robin Hood's Bay, nestling into the
cliffside, is well seen, while on the return Ravenscar's high cliffs can be
seen at their best.

Leave the car in Ravenscar village by the roadside near the National
Trust Information Centre (worth a visit) outside the grounds of the Raven
Hall Hotel, built on the site of a Roman signal station (GR 980 015) and
take the broad track sloping down past the front of the Centre. On the
way down ignore a tarmac drive on the right, but at the next fork keep
right (unless you wish to use the old railway track for your outward route,
which is more level but has fewer views, in which case fork left).

Immediately after a Cleveland Way marker post turn sharply back left
on an ascending path which crosses the old railway by a bridge. About 80
yards up the stony path past the bridge turn sharp right through a gate
into a field and walk forward for a few yards before bearing half-left uphill
to pass the end of a wall and reach a gate between two old railway
wagons. Walk straight up the next field, with the telegraph wires, towards
a bungalow, and cross a stile by the gate ahead. Turn right along the
tarmac road, which soon becomes a stony track. Ignore a fork beside a
bench on the left, but a few yards further on fork left to avoid the private
road to Brickyard Cottage. The track has now narrowed to a path. The
views seawards are superb. Keep along this level path, ignoring ascending
paths forking left, until you join a tarmac road on which you bear
right downhill.

Pass on the left old quarries, where alum was extensively mined; on the
right is the space to park cars used as the start of Walk 15. Just after this
at the fork keep right on the 1 in 4 downhill. Cross the old railway; this
is where you would need to leave the track if you had used it for the outward
leg — it is recognisable by a power line and the tall stone bridge crossed
by a tarmac road. Just after Stoupe Brow Cottage Farm a gap-stile on the
right with a Cleveland Way sign indicates our return route, but if
you want to visit the sands keep along the road to Stoupe Bank Farm,
from where there are steps down to the shore, then return to this point.

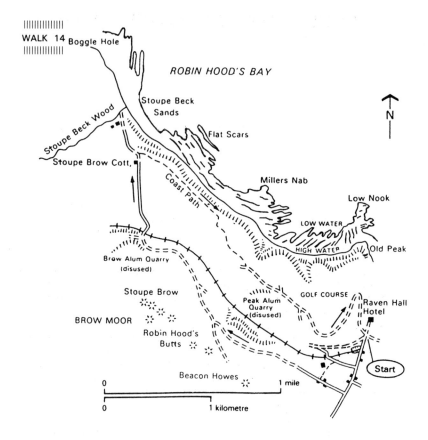

Having passed through the gap-stile no further directions are necessary, as the clear path follows the cliffs, until as it approaches Ravenscar it turns inland to a stile by a gate and you join a broad track. Turn left along this. Where the track forks, leave the Cleveland Way by keeping left on the branch which climbs and bears left past the golf course before curving right to pass below the crenellated wall of the hotel and return to the starting point.

ROBIN HOOD'S BAY AND RAMSDALE

WALK 15

★

7 miles (11 km)
Excluding Stoupe Brow 6 miles (9.5 km)
Note: If you wish to use the route along the sands,
check before you set off that the tide will be out.

The ancient fishing village of Robin Hood's Bay, clinging picturesquely
but precariously to the cliffside, is a must for all visitors to the North York
Moors, but as it gets very congested in the season and parking is
expensive, I have chosen to start the ramble at Stoupe Brow, where there
is plenty of free parking, and where walkers with time and energy might
like to combine the walk with Walk 14. The village itself is thus reached
midway through the ramble, and after a refreshment stop can be explored
at leisure before resuming the walk. But those who find themselves
already in Robin Hood's Bay can of course start the ramble there and
omit Stoupe Brow, and they should turn at once to [*] below.
     Motorists intending to leave the car at Stoupe Brow should take the
road north-west from the crossroads near the windmill at the top end of
Ravenscar (signposted Stoupe Brow) and after 1½ miles park the car by
the road side, below the old alum quarries, just before the road forks,
both branches being marked as no through roads (GR 960 023).

Walk down the tarmac road, crossing the old railway line, to Stoupe Brow
Cottage Farm, where the Cleveland Way joins your route over a stile on
the right. Keep on the road as far as Stoupe Bank Farm, then continue
downhill through the trees, soon by steps. If the tide is out, the walk to
Robin Hood's Bay could be on the sands and rocks of the beach. One
used also to be able to walk along the top of the cliffs, but erosion has
now made that unsafe (making a diversion of the Cleveland Way
necessary), so you must make a detour inland, before joining the cliff path
in time for the best view down to the village of Robin Hood's Bay. So
cross the concrete footbridge over Stoupe Beck and follow the path forking
left uphill. Pass through a gate and follow the path up to a field. Cross
over to the hedge ahead and turn left, keeping the hedge on your right.
     Soon you enter a hedged track, which is followed to a gate and a
tarmac lane. Boggle Hole youth hostel is down to the right, but we cross
straight over [†] along the tarmac road between houses. Follow the road
straight through between Mill Beck and South House Farms, passing
through a gate on the way, after which the road winds its way steeply
down to Mill Beck. Cross the footbridge and the stile and bear left to

47

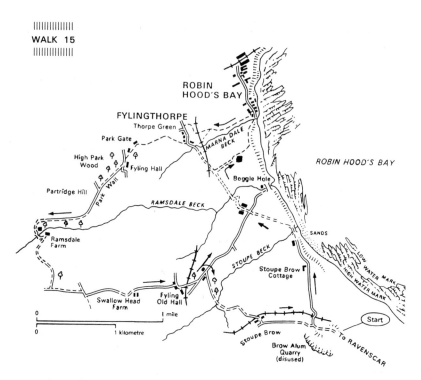

another stile, after which the path bears right to rejoin the road. Turn right uphill. At the top there are remnants of old paving and a bench with a pleasant view back. Cross the stile by the gate and follow the lane to the next junction, where you turn right along Mark Lane, a no through road.

Immediately before the gate into the Farsyde Riding Centre turn left and cross the stile into a fenced path. Leave this over another stile and bear slightly right over the car park to yet another stile in the far left-hand corner. A hedged path now leads to a kissing-gate at the cliff edge. Turn left along the cliff top path. The quaint romantic views of 'Bay', the short name for the village, soon come into sight. Follow the clear path until on the edge of the village you reach a less clear path forking right, with a sign 'To the Beach', which brings you down to the 'front'.

[*] When you have finished exploring the many nooks and crannies of the village, return to the slipway at the bottom of the village street, known as Way Foot. A few yards up on the left is Albion Road, where a sign points 'To the cliffs'. Walk up here, but instead of forking left up the steps to the cliffs, keep forward on the track, and when it turns right to a gate keep ahead on a clear path through the woods, with Marna Dale Beck down to the left. Cross a stile out of the wood, and a clear path leads forward, still parallel to the beck, soon with a hedge on the right. Pass through a gateway and keep on with the hedge to your right, following it

round until you cross a stile by a gate in a facing fence. Continue with the hedge to your right to cross another stile near the far right-hand corner of the field.

Follow the clear path to reach the old railway line and turn right along it, but only for 50 yards to a footpath signpost and stile on the left. Turn fairly sharp right across the next field to an oak tree and a small gate, then left along a narrow path between fences to the houses. Turn left along the road, ignoring Middlewood Close, but turning right into Middlewood Crescent and following it to its end, where there is a stile. Walk forward for a few yards to another stile, then turn right uphill with the hedge to your left, following the line of the overhead wires. Cross the stile in the top corner and keep along the hedge on your left uphill towards Park Gate Farm. When you reach a gate on the left a few yards after a footpath signpost, bear half-right across the field to the ladder-stile opposite. Bear left up the track in front of the cottages, and turn left at the T-junction to pass through a gate and along the front of the farm and its buildings on a stone flagged path, to another gate into the wood. Take an immediate right turn up some steps to a partly paved trod, which is on the site of an ancient park wall, and follow the path to a small gate and a tarmac road.

Turn left along the road, but just before reaching the fine residence of Fyling Hall, now a school, take the upper of two tracks forking half-right, a straight lane up through the trees, continuing the line of the old park wall. Soon you must ignore another track forking right and keep forward with the wall to your left. From time to time over the wall there are views of the Bay and Ravenscar. When the wood on the right ends there is a fork: bear left, and after 200 yards the trees on the left end too and you have a grand open view of Ramsdale. Pass a bungalow called Oakwood and soon enter Oak Wood, still on the wall road, which eventually winds down to the fast flowing Ramsdale Beck. Pass the old mill and cross the bridge over the beck, then bear left up to Ramsdale Mill Farm, where the track makes a hairpin bend to the right.

Pass through a gate into a field and walk along the right-hand edge of this with the wood to your right. This section can be wet and muddy. At the end of the field the track passes through another gate back into the wood. You are soon joined by another track from the left. Keep forward until you reach a junction by a footpath signpost: turn left for Fyling Old Hall. The track ends at a gate into another field: keep along with the wall to your right to the top corner of the field, where a signpost points right along a walled lane. Pass through a gate. Two bumps seen ahead, above the general line of the moor, are High Langdale End on the right and Broxa Forest on the left. The lane takes a left-hand turn and widens, soon emerging into a field. Opposite two gates on the left the track swings right across the field towards some gorse bushes, then bears left again to drop and pass through a gate just to the left of Swallow Head Farm.

Walk straight down through the yard on to a track which leads to another gate. Follow the farm access road to a motor road, where you turn right for Fyling Old Hall, a fine building in a lovely setting. The road then descends, crossing the line of the old railway (marked by steps on each side of the road) and a beck. At the top of the hill you are joined by another road from the right: keep forward (signposted 'Beach only'), and if you started the walk in Robin Hood's Bay and want to omit Stoupe Brow, follow the road down to where a tarmac road leaves it on the left towards houses, turn left along this and go back to [✝] above. Or if the tide is out and you want to return by the sands, follow the road all the way down to Boggle Hole and the beach. To return to Stoupe Brow take the signposted bridleway on the right between hedges, opposite a large house on the left.

Pass through a gate and keep left downhill at the fork. Cross Stoupe Beck by a footbridge and keep forward up the field to rejoin the track coming from the ford. It soon bears left through a gateway and becomes hedged again. Curve right at the top, now with the hedge only on the left, and soon bear left to a gate. Keep up the right-hand edge of the next field, bearing left at the top into a fenced track which leads to a gate on to the old railway line with Browside Farm ahead. Turn left along the railway track, enjoying once more the glorious views to the sea, and immediately after passing under a tall stone and brick bridge, fork left off the track to reach the motor road you walked down earlier. Turn left up it, over the bridge, to return to the car.

MALLYAN SPOUT

WALK 16

★

3½ miles (5.5 km)

There are several waterfalls around Goathland, of which Mallyan Spout is the best known. There is a free car park in Goathland just off the main road at the north-east corner of the village (GR 833 013).

From this walk past the conveniences along the road to Darnholm and Beck Hole for about 70 yards, before turning left off the road through a wicket gate by the side of a field gate into an enclosed footpath (signposted Grosmont Rail Trail), with houses on the right and a small ravine on the left. You are walking on the site of the original railway — a steep slope down to Beck Hole; the line was diverted after a fatal accident in 1865. Leave the old railway track at the road, soon encountered; turn to the right, walking as far as the crossroads (notice the old paving stones by the side of the road) where turn left (towards Beck Hole); turn right just before the first house, into an enclosed footpath (signposted). Cross a stile into a field and follow the right-hand edge of the field down to a stile at the bottom on the right. Below you will see the railway line winding its way through the gorge and you should hear the rushing water of Eller Beck.

Over the stile, bear right down the steps cut into the steep slope, cross the footbridge and pass beneath the railway bridge. The water passes through a narrow rock channel into a deep pool. Resist the temptation to jump the channel; be warned by the nearby memorial to a 16 year old boy who in 1908 was accidentally drowned.

Follow the footpath with the fence and beck to your left. Before the next railway bridge, which you will soon see down on your left, you will hear the sound of Water Ark Foss, another of the waterfalls, but access is dangerously steep and not to be recommended. Continue up the path to a bench, there bearing slightly right to follow the wall and hedge on the left. Pass to the right of a cottage and make for Hill House Farm ahead, but 60 yards before it bear left off the track on a narrow path to pass beneath power lines towards a wall on the left. Follow the wall to the farm access road and keep left down this, with a deep gorge and the railway line down to your left.

At the road turn left over the railway bridge. By the bench overlooking the picturesque hamlet of Beck Hole take the footpath descending steeply left. At the foot a signpost points left to Thomason Foss, another of the waterfalls, and you might like to make a detour to visit it. Having

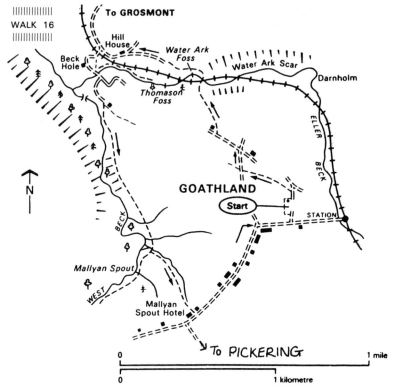

To GROSMONT

Hill House

Water Ark Foss

Water Ark Scar

Beck Hole

Darnholm

Thomason Foss

ELLER BECK

GOATHLAND

Start

STATION

BECK

Mallyan Spout

WEST

Mallyan Spout Hotel

To PICKERING

N

0   1 mile

0   1 kilometre

returned to this point turn left at the road to cross Eller Beck; pass the Birch Hall Inn, a free house which also doubles as a shop, and take a right turn just past it (signposted) through a gate into a lane. Pass through another gate on which is a notice 'Private. No access for vehicles. Public footpath'. Turn left and, opposite Incline Cottage, (we are at the foot of the old railway incline) pass through a gate on the right displaying a notice 'To the Mallyan'.

Now the path is beside West Beck at first; go through a kissing-gate; as soon as the woods are reached the path starts to rise and steps zigzag steeply up. The tree-covered gorge is down on the right, deciduous trees on this side, mixed on the other — not only deciduous with conifers, but the conifers are themselves varied, thus avoiding monotony. The uphill track continues above the trees until the houses of Goathland can be seen. Then the way descends steeply by the edge of the wood. Go over a little beck on a wooden footbridge; go steeply down, almost to water level; cross another small stream by a bridge and follow the wooden catwalk.

Soon you will reach a track coming in from the left. A bench marks the spot and there is a signpost pointing straight on to Mallyan Spout and left up to Goathland. This will be our return route, but first continue forward for a very short distance, at first on a wide path. Negotiate some rocks beneath steep cliffs. Suddenly, on the left, coming down from the cliff top, is Mallyan Spout. The height is impressive but the amount of water may disappoint, because the stream feeding West Beck is only a small one.

There is a path straight ahead, which follows West Beck to the next road bridge, where one can turn left to return to Goathland, but it tends to be muddy, the rocks are slippery and there are some awkward sections. So I suggest you return to the signpost and bear right up to Goathland, there emerging by the side of the Mallyan Hotel. Turn left through the village to return to the car.

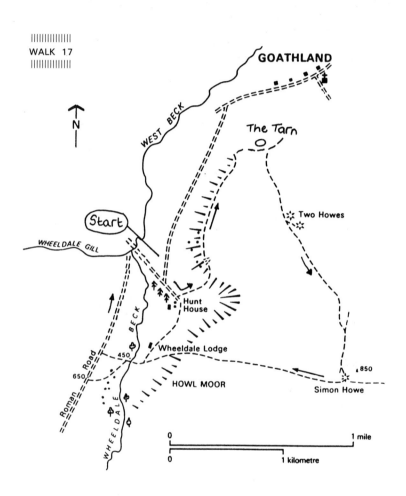

||||||||||||||||
WALK 17
||||||||||||||||

GOATHLAND

WEST BECK

The Tarn

N

Start

WHEELDALE GILL

Two Howes

Hunt House

BECK

Roman Road

450

Wheeldale Lodge

650

HOWL MOOR

850

Simon Howe

WHEELDALE

0   1 mile

0   1 kilometre

TWO HOWES, SIMON HOWE, WHEELDALE BECK AND THE ROMAN ROAD

WALK 17

★

4 miles (6.5 km)

A moorland stroll followed by a visit to the most famous Roman remains in the North York Moors. From the southern end of the village of Goathland take the road signposted to Egton Bridge, soon forking left off it along a no through road signposted to 'Hunt House and the Roman Road'. About 50 yards before you reach a wood there is plenty of roadside parking (GR 814 989).

Walk on along the road, passing to the left of the wood, as far as Hunt House on the right. Now the greatest attention must be paid to route-finding! Just before the track crosses a beck and opposite a small garden gate on the right there are two large stones on the left (and a bridleway sign) which enable you to cross the roadside ditch: cross these and bear sharp left, back in the direction you have just come, with the ditch between you and the track. Climb slightly at an acute angle to the track, to find a clear narrow path through the bracken: IT IS ESSENTIAL TO FIND THIS PATH, unmistakable in its clarity. Ignore cross paths, and when you reach an open grassy area with patches of heather, cross straight over, but look slightly right at the far side to find the continuation of the narrow path through the bracken. The path heads towards a stony ridge on the skyline. When you reach it climb up through the rocks to a clear cross path: turn left along this.

Now you have leisure to enjoy the views. Look right across the moor: the prominent cairn on the horizon will be passed on our return route. The clear path, marked by a series of cairns, keeps along the top of the rocky ridge: avoid all temptations to fork left on to descending paths, particularly one leading to a well-built cairn in front of an old quarry. After some time you reach a ravine with a stretch of water in it: this is The Tarn, the turning point of our walk. Keep the ravine and tarn to your left and about halfway along the tarn you will reach a clear path forking right up across the heather moor with a cairn near the start; follow this path. (If you want to continue to Goathland, keep on to the end of the tarn and there bear left.)

The path leads to the Two Howes, prominent cairns on tumuli, two of the thousands of ancient burial mounds on the moors. About 40 yards past the first one on the way to the second a clear path forks right, which leads to the large cairn on Simon Howe, a mile away on the skyline, with the trig point some way to the left. At this cairn turn right on to the clear descending path over Howl Moor, part of the route of the Lyke Wake Walk, which you follow all the way down to the track at the bottom leading from Wheeldale Lodge youth hostel to Wheeldale Beck, crossing over another clear track on the way down.

Bear left, cross a stile and then Wheeldale Beck by stepping stones, and climb steeply up the other side, bearing half-left at the signpost on a path slanting up through the bracken. You now reach the excavated section of the Roman road, part of a road connecting the fort at Malton with the coast near Whitby, probably used in late Roman times as a link with the signal stations on the coast. The large stones now visible formed the raised central foundation and were originally covered by a finer road surface, probably of gravel. Explore this as far as you like along to the left, but the route of your walk turns right along it to a gate in the next cross wall.

Cross the ladder-stile by the gate and continue following the route of the road. The excavated section ends just before another cross wall with a gate in it. Go through the gate and continue down with a wall to your right to a stile in the next corner of the field, then bear half-left on to a descending track and follow it down through the middle of the field, passing a footpath sign on the way. When the track forks near the bottom, ignore the right-hand branch leading to a gate and keep forward downhill towards the beck. Bear right at the bottom to cross a stile, ignore the first footbridge on the left and follow the path along until it ends at another footbridge. Cross this and turn right along the track, which leads back to the car.

THE VALLEY OF THE MURK ESK

WALK 18

★

6 miles (9.5 km)

The Murk Esk begins at the confluence of West Beck and Eller Beck at Beck Hole and ends where it joins the Esk at Grosmont (pronounced Growmont) two miles away as the crow flies. There can be few shorter rivers and few lovelier, winding as it does through woodlands and meadows chosen by George Stephenson for the line of the first Whitby to Pickering railway, opened in 1836 as a horse drawn tramway. It was bought by George Hudson, the 'Railway King' in 1845 and improved to take steam locomotives, remaining in regular use until 1865, when it was replaced by a new line along the valley side. Now this is used by the private and very popular North Yorkshire Moors Railway from Pickering to Grosmont, where today it links up with British Rail's Esk Valley line to Whitby.

We start our walk at the large Grosmont car park and picnic site, set in woodland opposite the football field on the road to Egton (GR 825 053) (honesty box). Walk back up the road towards the village, under the railway bridge (there are toilets here) and over the level crossing at the station. Immediately after this turn right through the gate, cross the footbridge over the Murk Esk and fork slightly left uphill (the track straight ahead leads through a tunnel to the loco sheds) past the school and church to a kissing-gate and track: bear right along it (signposted 'Rail Trail'). In a few yards go through another gate and 50 yards further on there is a bench on the right with a fine view to Grosmont and the Esk valley. Opposite it on the left is another gate and signpost 'Rail Trail'. Through this, follow the path to another gate and descend with it to join the railway to Pickering. Soon you pass through a kissing-gate and bear right along a grit track, which is in fact the line of the older railway. Soon the present railway bears off left and we reach the cottages and former chapel at Esk Valley.

Keep straight ahead through the gate, still on the old railway track. Cross the Murk Esk by a metal footbridge and keep on along the old railway, here a broad grassy way. Cross a stile into woodland. A short distance further on the railway recrossed the river (only the abutments of the old bridge survive), but ignore the new footbridge and stay on this side, on a footpath which climbs by steps. After crossing a stile you reach a fork, where one signpost points right to Egton Bridge and Egton and another also points right to Goathland by the Rail Trail, but your route

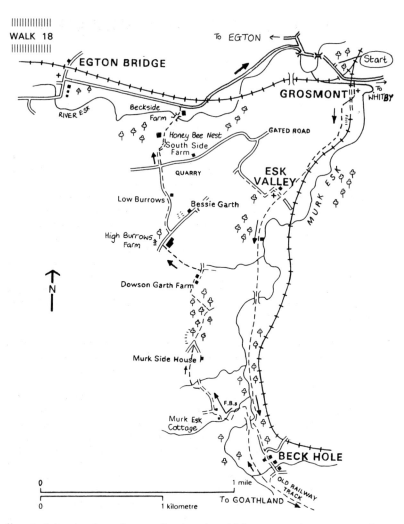

lies straight ahead on the woodland path, which soon reaches a gate and the motor road. Bear right through the lovely hamlet of Beck Hole.

Cross Eller Beck by the road bridge, and just after the Birch Hall Inn follow the public bridleway sign pointing right through a gate down a track. Pass through another gate to return to the line of the old railway. Turning left would take you to Goathland, but you turn right along it, ignoring a bridleway straight ahead. Cross Eller Beck again by enormous stepping-stones (the new footbridge is much less fun!) and read the two notices to the left of the track about the history of the old railway. Continue along the old track. Ignore a signpost pointing right down some steps (Grosmont. Rail Trail) and keep forward across the river bridge and through a gate. In just over 100 yards fork left off the track onto a clear path leading to a gate with the sign 'Egton'.

Ignore a footbridge on the right (signposted 'Grosmont') and keep straight on (signposted 'Egton'), in a few yards crossing a broader bridge. Cross another bridge and keep up with the beck to your right, soon crossing it by yet another bridge. Turn left for a few yards then bear half-right uphill on to a clear track which leads up to the right of a ruined building then bears left to Murk Esk Cottage. Go through the gate to the left of the house and turn sharp right to pass behind it and to the left of a stone outbuilding, there bearing slightly left to pass through an old gateway and up a track to a footpath sign ahead. Here bear slightly left, now the path is faint, and head for a gate in the wall ahead.

The next section of path has been diverted away from Murk Side House. Pass through the gate and leave the track to climb half-left on a faint path through bracken. Soon you reach a marker post which points you slightly right over a shallow valley. Having crossed this, bear slightly left fairly steeply uphill, and you will soon see a gate with a yellow waymark in a facing wall. Murk Side House is well below you to the right and there is a fine view over the valley of the Murk Esk. Pass through the gate and walk straight forward across the next large field to the next gate at the far side. Here the diversion ends. Cross the farm access road to another gate and keep forward along a grassy track. Shortly before the end of the wood the track forks and a waymark points you left uphill. Immediately the track levels out take a path slanting sharply back on the right which leads to a stile on the edge of the wood with Dowson Garth Farm ahead.

At present the next field has a quantity of rusty machinery in it. Walk towards the farm and pass through a gateway in the wall ahead. Following the track, pass to the left of the first stone barn, kink right and then left, now with a large modern barn to your left, at the end of this kink left and then right, following the track through the yard, which you leave by a gate at the far end. Walk forward for 20 yards, then fork half-left off the track through a gate and bear left uphill along the edge of the field with a fence to your left. There is a fine view back and to the right. In the top corner of the field cross the stile and keep forward with the hedge now to your right. Keeping to the left of High Burrows Farm, walk forward into the trees to find a step-stile in the wall ahead.

Ignoring the public footpath opposite, turn right along the road for 100 yards to the next footpath sign on the left. Go through the gate and along the track with a wall to your right. Follow the track to the left of Low Burrows Farm and through a gate into a field. Keep down the right-hand edge of the field to the next gate, then down the left-hand edge of the next one to a gate at the bottom and a minor road. Cross this diagonally right and go through a gate marked 'Honey Bee Nest'. There is a grand view over the Esk valley, with Egton on the hill beyond. Walk down the steep access road to the house. Pass to the right of this, through a gate into a field, and keep on down the right-hand edge of this to a stile by a gate at the foot. Now bear right for a few yards, then left across a beck, then right alongside the beck to a footbridge over the river Esk.

Bear left uphill to the stile by the gate on the left of the white house of Beckside Farm and keep forward for 20 yards to join a clear cross-track. Turn right along this. Soon you pass Toll Cottage, with a notice of the tolls which used to be payable on this old road, which is still private but is now a permissive footpath. Pass under the Esk valley railway. At the motor road bear right, then left to cross the Esk by the road bridge, and your starting point is a short distance along on the left.

EGTON GRANGE

★

4 miles (6.5 km)

In the little known valley of Egton Grange, so short as apparently not to warrant the dignity of the name 'dale', peace and quiet may easily be found with little effort.

Leave Egton Bridge by the road south of the river Esk and keep right at the fork past the Horseshoe Hotel on the Rosedale road. Park the car 400 yards further on, on the verge by the side of Butter Beck between the covered ford and the cottage further south on the other side of the road (GR 796 048). Walk past the cottage (Peat House) and just before the 1:3 steep hill sign fork left over the bridge up the lane (public bridleway sign).

Pass between Hall Grange farmhouse and its buildings and continue on the farm road, crossing several cattle grids, and after you have passed to the left of a fairly large wood the view opens out and you see Grange Head Farm ahead. When the track makes a sharp turn right to the farm go through the gate on the left.

Now for a short distance attention must be paid to route-finding. You enter a large area of rough pasture, criss-crossed with tracks and ditches. It is probably easiest to head straight up from the gate, bearing slightly right, for about 300 yards, when you will hit a beck coming straight down the hillside, with the remains of a wall to the right of it, looking like a grassy embankment. Continue up, keeping this beck to your right, but where the gradient eases and the ditch and wall bear right, keep straight forward towards two old gateposts in the fence ahead. Cross the stile beside these and walk forward for 40 yards to meet an indistinct cross track. Turn left along this, in a few yards crossing through a hollow way, and continue forward, parallel to the fence/wall about 30 yards to your left. The track is at times little more than a footpath. Soon a motor road comes into view ahead and in the distance Whitby Abbey and the sea. When the wall on your left bears left, you join a track which passes to the right of a stone shooting butt, the last of a line; follow it to the narrow tarmac road (from Egton to Stape).

Turn left along the road and keep left at the next fork, passing between two standing stones. The road begins to descend, swings right to pass a quarry and then left again. About 400 yards further on, on a slight right-hand bend, take the broad track on the left (bridleway sign). Where the track bears left to Swang Farm, keep straight ahead along a grassy track

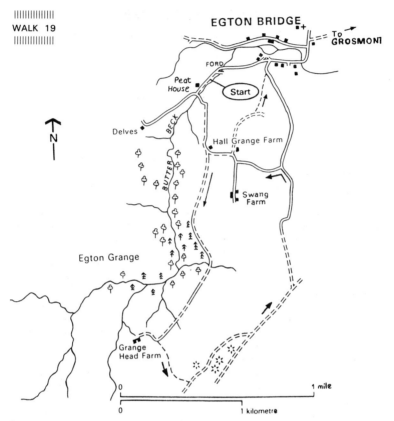

between hedges. Go through a gate ahead (Hall Grange Farm is down to the left) and pass some yards to the left of a dilapidated barn, again along a grassy track between hedges. Pass through another gate. Soon the track bears slightly right and narrows, with a wall and tall holly hedge to the right and a wall to the left, over which is a fine view of Eskdale. Cross a stile by a gate and continue gently down on the grassy track, which swings left and then right again.

Immediately before the track crosses a beck, pass through the gate on the left and walk downhill with the hedge and beck to your right, soon crossing a step-stile ahead and continuing down, ignoring a stile in the fence on the right, with the beck still to your right. Keep down until just below a mass of blackthorn on the right you turn right (the beck has now disappeared) along the bottom edge of this hedge for 40 yards to a facing wall with a gap in it. Ignore this and bear left down with the wall on your right to a stile in the bottom corner of the field leading to a hedged track and the motor road. Turn left down the road and left at the next junction by the Horseshoe Hotel to return to the car.

62

BEGGAR'S BRIDGE
AND EAST ARNECLIFF WOOD

WALK 20

3 miles (5 km)

Although often muddy, this is a walk which should not be missed, taking in as it does some fine scenery of the river Esk passing through one of its most spectacular gorges, caused chiefly by the meltwaters of the North Sea Glacier. This series of deep gorges makes Eskdale unlike most other Yorkshire dales in that it has no road following the valley bottom. Park by the delightful 17th century Beggar's Bridge below the village of Glaisdale, a spot rather spoilt by the modern road and railway bridges (GR 784 054).

Cross Glaisdale Beck by the footbridge beside the ford (signposted 'Coast to Coast: Esk Valley Walk') and ascend the stepped path into the wood. Follow this lovely woodland path, paved for part of its length, all the way to the next motor road, where you turn left downhill. Coming to the valley bottom, the road goes alongside Butter Beck (the starting point for Walk 19). Immediately after the Horseshoe Hotel in Egton Bridge bear half-left over the hotel's access road to find behind a railing a flagged path

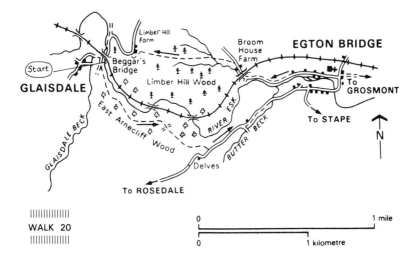

63

leading to stepping stones over the river. The first set of stones leads to an island, the second set to the far bank; walk up some steps to reach the motor road where you turn left.

After a section by the river the road goes under the railway and passes Broom House Farm. About 100 yards further on at the end of the wood on the left, go left across a stile by a gate and walk along the top edge of the wood. After the wood ends the path drops and bears left to cross a beck, then bears right quite steeply uphill to a stile into the wood ahead. A ride through the wood takes you to a stile and the right-hand side of a hedge bordering a field. Cross the next stile in the far corner and keep forward on the track across the next field. About 70 yards before Limber Hill Farm, at a hedge corner on the left, bear half-left off the track and follow the hedge on your left along, passing a telegraph pole, to a gate in the far corner. Through this turn sharp right to another gate on to the motor road and turn left downhill, bearing left again when you reach the river to return to the car.

LOWER GLAISDALE

WALK 21

★

5½ miles (9 km)

Glaisdale is a scattered village, chiefly on the hillside at the junction of the dale with the same name with Eskdale. It was once an ironstone mining centre, with records of this activity going back to the 13th century, and even in the mid-19th century there were three blast furnaces here. The scene is now completely pastoral, but added interest may be found in the sturdily built cottages in the village, the shapes of old weathered scars and the green track of an old quarry railway, which we shall use on the return journey.

Park below Glaisdale at Beggar's Bridge (see Walk 20) and cross Glaisdale

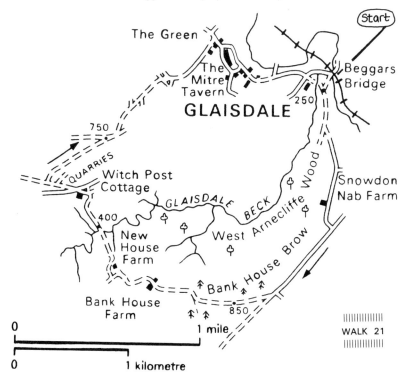

Beck by the footbridge beside the ford, continuing up the track marked as 'Unsuitable for Motors'. In 100 yards at the fork keep left, and soon after keep left at another fork, where the right branch goes through a metal gate. The track now becomes narrower and ascends; it is tarmac from Snowdon Nab Farm. When you reach the motor road turn right along it.

Thirty yards after crossing a cattle grid bear half-right on a very good green moorland track through the heather and continue forward along Bank House Brow Plantation. Go over a stile by a gate into the wood, taking a forward track sloping down through the trees. Pass through a gateway and continue along the bottom edge of the wood until you see a gate in the wall on the right opposite a small stile into the wood on the left. Go through and walk down the field with the wall to your right. There is an old hollow way which soon bears left: follow it down to Bank House Farm, enjoying the glorious view of lower Glaisdale. Enter the farmyard through a gate, walk through the yard and continue along the track, which bears right and then left to reach the tarmac road through a gate.

Turn right along the road, passing to the left of New House Farm, and cross the valley floor. Join the up-dale road at Witch Post Cottage and bear left, but after a few yards bear half-right on a road which initially is tarred but soon becomes a dirt track. Go over the stile by a gate across the track, continuing forward until just before the track crosses a small stone bridge, where you turn right towards the disused quarry, bearing left at a fork soon afterwards and passing to the left of the quarry. The green track through the bracken is now on the site of the old railway, taking a straight course until it reaches the Glaisdale Rigg road at an embankment before a cutting. Leave the line of the railway and join the road on your left, following it down to The Green in Glaisdale (a grassy area with a bench).

Turn right on joining the main road, but in 50 yards fork left by the village hall down a narrow tarmac path. On reaching the next road turn left downhill on the raised walkway, and where this ends continue down the narrow road. Rejoin the main road at the Arncliffe Arms and turn left to complete the circuit.

LITTLE FRYUP DALE

WALK 22

★

7 miles (11.5 km)

Danby comprises several communities, the village to the north of the river Esk being known as Danby End, the part to the south being Ainthorpe, today's starting point. On Danby Rigg, which we shall cross, there are more than 800 cairns, probably Bronze Age, and on Danby High Moor, which we shall leave on our right, a settlement of ancient origin. Canon Atkinson was vicar here for 53 years; among other things he wrote *Forty Years in a Moorland Parish*, for us a useful work of reference, published in 1891. After crossing the Rigg the intention is to pass through the head of the romantic Little Fryup Dale; along the top on the other side, known as Heads; returning in Eskdale through Crag Wood and via Duck Bridge, an ancient monument.

Motoring, take the road in Ainthorpe signposted Fryup to pass the Fox and Hounds and the village green. Look out for roadside parking soon after starting to climb up the Rigg (GR 704 076). Walking, continue up the road, passing tennis courts on both sides, and just before it bends left fork right along a signposted bridleway. The path leads through a gate and passes to the left of an old quarry. A large upright stone in a circle of small stones, strongly marked with weather channels and incised with a big 'T' is also passed. Tumuli are all around. It is not long before you reach the lip of the moor and a fine view of Little Fryup Dale, with a glimpse of Great Fryup Dale through Fairy Cross Plain lying between the south end of Heads and the smooth pimple of Round Hill.

The track slopes down towards Crossley House. You reach the tarmac at a junction: keep forward on the road which descends to cross the head of the valley. Walk over a cattle grid and pass some neat cottages and Stonebeck Gate Farm, and when you have passed one field beyond the farm, go through a gate into a green lane on the left. At the next gate across the track turn immediately right along another walled lane. Pass through a gate at the end, at a triangular conifer copse, from which take a look at the heads of both Fryup dales, for you are now in line with the dividing Round Hill.

Turn left on a good path emerging from the conifers onto the open moor, with a wall and green fields to the left. Pass another group of conifers, continuing forward but sloping up towards the top of Heads. When the path has reached its highest point it continues on the whole parallel to the edge of the escarpment but about 100 yards in from it, not

always clearly defined. Soon you will see that you are heading for a wall in the distance; pass through a gate at the escarpment end of this wall and keep forward with a wall to your left (there is no path at this point). Crag Wood and Danby Crag are over the wall. Follow it to another gate, after which it becomes a fence, with Head House Farm now visible ahead. Follow the fence down to a gate, well to the left of the farm, with a fine view of Eskdale ahead.

Follow the track downhill. When you are below the farm, look for a track forking sharp left and going steeply downhill to join a cross track lower down, on which you bear left; or, if you want a final view of Great Fryup Dale, keep forward on a grassy track (avoid bearing right up to the farm) until another track comes down from the farm, look right for the Dale, then bear sharp left on the descending track. Keep forward and soon you have a wall to your right which leads to a gate into Crag Wood. Follow the clear path through the wood, noticing the remains of paving in places. Leave the wood through a gate and walk forward to a footpath sign, there continuing forward and dropping to cross a farm track to a gate ahead into a short section of lane which leads to the access road from Crag Farm which is to your right.

Keep forward along the access road and cross the river Esk, wide upstream and downstream but narrow and rushing below the substantial bridge. Continue on this road as far as the main dale road, on which turn left. This is one of the few places in Eskdale where there is a road in the valley bottom: usually the steep-sided narrow valley made road-making too difficult. About 600 yards further on the road forks: take the minor road straight on to Duck Bridge, a fine old bridge, steep and narrow.

On the other side EITHER turn to the left, pass the remains of Danby Castle, turn right at the T-junction and follow the road back to the car, OR fork right along the road, noticing the old paving in places to the left of it, and a few yards past a large house on the right cross the signposted stile on the left and follow the fenced path along the edge of the field. Ignore a kissing-gate on the left signposted 'Castle Footpath', cross the stile straight ahead and bear right round the edge of the field. Cross another stile and keep forward, now with a wall to your right, parallel to a line of power line poles. At the end of the field cross a stile on the left and continue up the fenced track, crossing another stile into a walled lane which leads you back to Ainthorpe. Turn left up the road to return to the car.

GREAT FRYUP HEAD

WALK 23

★

5 miles (8 km)

The hub of the National Park is surely Rosedale Head, readily accessible to the motorist from north and south. Here are lots of landmarks, such as the Old Margery Stone; crowds of crosses such as White Cross (or Fat Betty) and, most famous of all, Ralph Cross East with the hollow top for the leaving of alms for travellers; valuable viewpoints of Rosedale, Westerdale and Danby Dale; easy access to those dales, also to Farndale and, for the walker, Great and Little Fryup Dales.

The scenery at the head of Great Fryup Dale is quite splendid, with crags and shapely hills, delightful becks and waterfalls, surrounded by heather moors. This is a beautiful ramble on easy tracks and paths, but towards the end **there is an exceedingly steep climb**.

Just over a mile along the road to Rosedale from the Ralph Crosses at a junction with a minor road there is a signpost showing Castleton 6, Rosedale 3, Pickering 13. The signpost does not say where the road is going to, but it is to Little Fryup Dale. Follow this minor road for about 700 yards, and leave the car at the first junction, with a rough moor road to the right (public bridleway sign), leading past Trough House, a stone shooting house the roof of which can be seen (GR 700 019).

Walk along the rough road, and when you have passed to the right of Trough House you will see signs of old pits on both sides. The track becomes a little damp as you round the head of the first of many streamlets feeding Great Fryup Beck. Continue on the track through heather, bilberry and bracken, noting a large cairn on the left which you will revisit on the return journey. Immediately beyond the cairn, but lower down on the left, is George Gap Spa, a chalybeate spring, which you can visit on your return up the valley.

Once you have rounded the head of the valley the path seems to fork and there is a wet section: the main branch, slanting gently up the hillside, keeps to the left of a deepish, rush-filled trough. Once you get a little higher up you are on a clear dry track again. Follow it all the way to the Glaisdale Rigg road, from where there is a good view of Glaisdale.

Now you must be careful for a few moments about route-finding. Stand with your back to the road facing the moor over which you have just come. There are two stony tracks, with a bridleway sign pointing along them to Trough House. Walk along the right-hand of these tracks for 50 yards, where there is a small cairn in the heather to the right of the

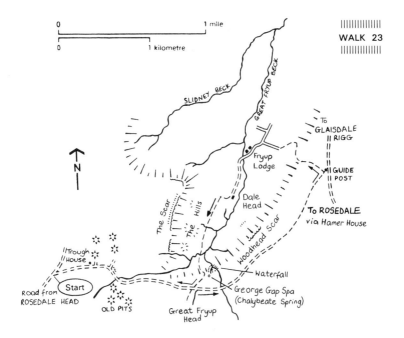

track. Two yards beyond the cairn fork right off the track and walk at right-angles to it across the moor: there is no clear path at first, but in about 30 yards you will reach a clear, narrow path heading forward and downhill; another cairn on the way down shows that you are on the right route. The path leads down to a gate in a cross wall by a holly tree from where there is a magnificent view of Great Fryup Dale.

Slope down right, at first in a hollow way, through trees. Follow the path as it makes a sharp turn left and descends to a gate into a walled lane. Walk down this and turn left along the road at the bottom. Follow it past Fryup Lodge, pass through a gate, cross Great Fryup Beck by a bridge and bear left on the track overlooking the lovely, tree-hung stream. Here you have a better look at the east side of the valley, topped by Wood Head Scar, another fine bit of country.

On reaching the buildings of Dale Head, now unoccupied, take the gate on the right and pass to the right of the buildings. About 30 yards after the track passes between two trees leave it at right-angles on the right, on an old grassy track climbing steeply, soon with a hedge and reed-filled dip to the left. Pass through a gap in the broken cross wall, cross the wooden stile and turn left along the clear track. Soon it peters out and you must fork right on a clear path. This area for obvious reasons is known as The Hills. For a short distance you have a wall to your left. Keep forward towards the head of the valley on a path which is clear most of the time.

Pass through a gate in a cross wall a few yards to the left of a

71

corrugated iron shelter. The path now bears half-left and drops to cross the beck by large stones, a lovely spot for a picnic. Now comes the hard work, for you must find the clear path up the daunting hillside ahead. After crossing the beck keep forward for a few yards then turn sharp right, steeply uphill on a clear path. (Before you do this it is worth making a short detour to look at a waterfall: instead of turning sharp right keep straight forward, soon crossing another beck; at the end of a short stretch of old wall on the left ignore the path forking left, and keep forward towards the coomb ahead — there is no clear path — for a view of the waterfall tumbling down the cliff on the right. Now return by the same route.)

The clear path leads uphill with the beck at first down to the right, but it soon bears gently left away from it — ignore a clear grassy track on your right here and make for the escarpment ahead. When you reach the top of the first slope look straight ahead up the valley and you will see your path zigzagging up to the left of the beck. So walk forward, cross the beck, and bear right on the clear path up the slope with the beck down to your right. Now you cannot lose your way, as you zigzag steeply uphill. When you reach grass, divert left to have a look at the chalybeate spring, distinctly coloured by deposits of iron. Then return to the path and follow it up to the large cairn you met on the outward route. Turn right along the track to return past Trough House to the car.

DANBY HIGH MOOR
AND BOTTON VILLAGE

WALK 24

★

6 miles (9.5 km)

The Camphill Village Trust runs a centre for the mentally handicapped, occupying almost the whole of the head of Danby Dale. As their introductory pack explains, 'The beautiful countryside provides a serene backdrop to the working community of Botton. Five farms, a bakery, printing press, creamery and food centre, as well as workshops producing wooden toys, beeswax candles, dolls, engraved glassware and woven goods guarantee that there is an interesting job for everyone, whatever their ability. Social life for the 300 people who live in Botton Village revolves around the 27 households where extended families of up to 16 people live . . . At Botton no one receives a wage and we try to be as self-sufficient as possible.' Today's ramble explores the lovely valley where this community lives.

Park at the junction with the minor road, one and a half miles from the Ralph Crosses where the signpost shows Rosedale 3, Pickering 13 and Castleton 6 (GR 697 012). Walk along the minor tarmac road over Danby High Moor for one and a half miles. When the road begins to descend on a long straight stretch you will see Danby Botton (Botton means a rounded valley) on the left and (if the weather is good) above it on the skyline the tip of Roseberry Topping more than 11 miles away. Down dale is Castleton, the chief village of upper Eskdale. Over to the left, on the other side of the valley, is Castleton Rigg, on which you may see cars moving along the road. When the Fryup Dales come into sight on the right there is a public bridleway sign on each side of the road. Ignore these, but 250 yards further on, opposite a grassy area on the right, there is another bridleway sign on the left. Follow the track, with the tumulus of Wolf Pit on the left.

The track soon narrows to a footpath which bears slightly right and gradually descends to the moor edge, where the valley is spread out at your feet. The path continues by slanting down the hillside, at first in a dip. It goes below crags and to the top side of a wood, 100 yards beyond which is a bridleway sign pointing left through a gate. Walk down the right-hand edge of the field, through a gate and straight forward down the metalled road past Botton Farm. Here you may choose between routes (a) or (b).

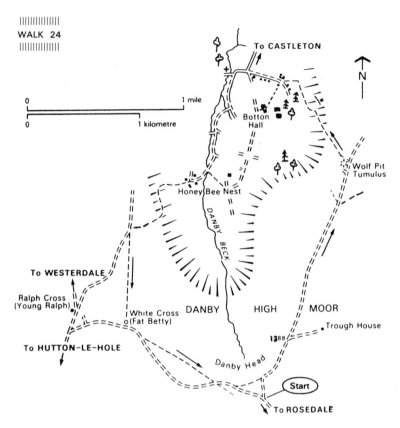

Route (a): Go straight down the road, descending the steep hill and at the crossroads keeping straight forward, ignoring the road on the left to the village centre. At the next fork by the beck keep left on the no through road signposted to Honey Bee Nest. Shortly after passing a large maintenance workshop on the right fork right (again signposted Honey Bee Nest Farm) over the beck. Ignore a left fork to High Farm and a right fork to Nook House and keep on along the road by Danby Beck. There are masses of daffodils here in April. When a paved path comes steeply down the hillside from the left, take the footpath on the right, parallel to the road. Here routes (a) and (b) rejoin.

Route (b) will be preferred by most, because it takes you through Botton Village centre. Descend the road for a short distance, but just past 'The Cottage' on the left turn left along a paved path signposted 'Village Centre'. When the path forks by a lamppost keep left through a gate. On reaching the next tarmac road the creamery and food centre (well worth a visit; I particularly like the cheeses!) are to the left, but our walk goes right past a map of the community and a box with a free information pack about it. At the T-junction ignore the kissing-gate straight ahead and turn left along the tarmac road. Cross a wooden road bridge and take the right fork, then at the next T-junction keep forward along another paved path. At the High Farm complex of buildings cross straight over a tarmac track and keep forward along another tarmac track. Pass through a gate and cross right to another kissing-gate and paved path signposted 'candleshop; press', which goes downhill to join the dale road on the valley floor. Cross the road and go left on the footpath parallel to the road. Here routes (a) and (b) rejoin.

When the path rejoins the road at Honey Bee Nest walk forward uphill towards the farm, ignoring a road forking left and passing the candleshop on the left. Bear left through the farmyard, along the back of the farmhouse, through a gate, then bear right past the end of a large shed to another gate, from where you follow the track steeply uphill to another gate straight ahead (don't bear left with the track to the gate in the field corner by some trees). Continue steeply uphill with a wall to your left: the path is actually in a deeply hollowed way, which leads to a gate out onto the open moor. Bear left along a footpath at first parallel to the top edge of the fields, climbing gently, soon with a hollow way to your right. Where this bears right and climbs straight up the hillside, your path follows suit. When you reach an old quarry keep straight on to pass to the left of it on a narrow path up to the road.

Turn left along the road. The Ralph Crosses can be seen on the skyline, but we follow the road for only a short distance, to where a bridleway sign on the left, across a ditch, close to a boundary stone points half-left over the moor. The path is clear as it heads for the next boundary stone on the skyline (don't miss the fine view back as you climb), and in fact there is a whole line of these stones, inscribed D on the Danby parish side and W on the Westerdale parish side, which you follow over the brow of the moor to reach 'Fat Betty', a white boundary stone marked 'White Cross' on the OS map, and the road.

Turn left along the road. On the right is Rosedale Head; the Lion Inn on Blakey Ridge can be seen beyond. Soon the road bears right and just after this a track forks left off it, heading towards another boundary stone 250 yards ahead. This is a short cut, but after rain it can be extremely boggy, so you may prefer to keep to the road. It leads back to the road, with the car a short distance to the left.

WALK 25

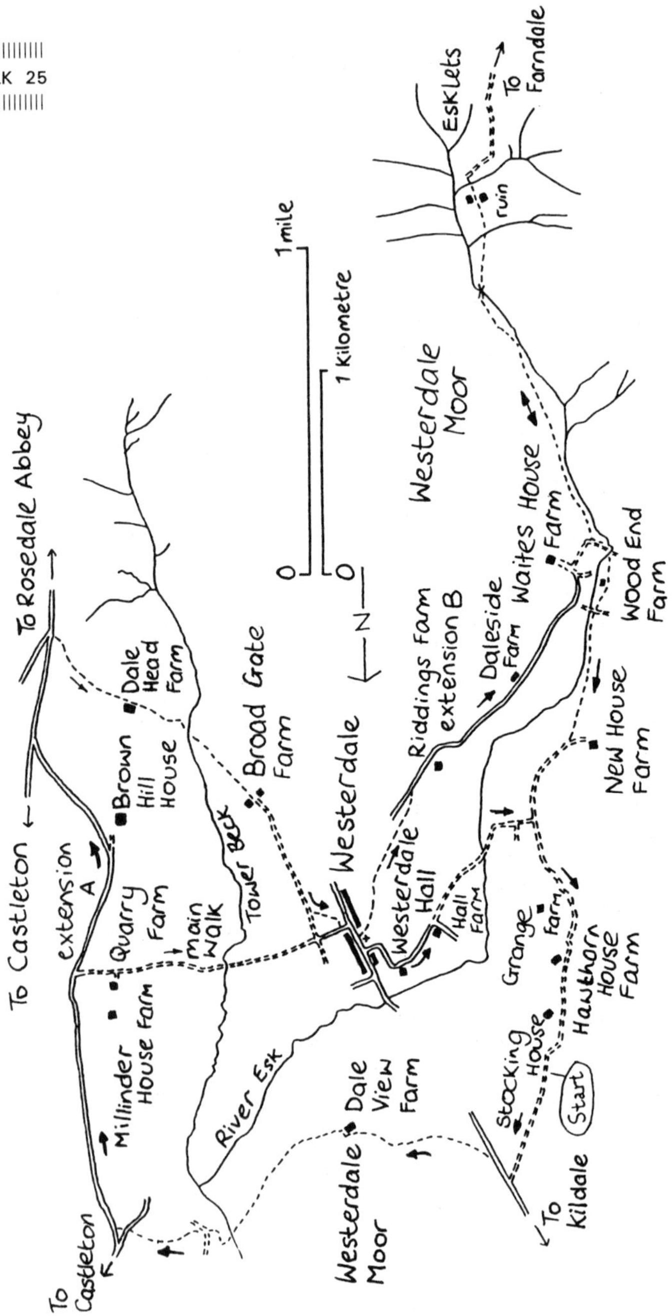

To Rosedale Abbey
To Castleton
extension A
Brown Hill House
Dale Head Farm
Broad Gate Farm
Quarry Farm
main walk
Tower Beck
Millinder House Farm
River Esk
To Castleton
Westerdale Moor
Dale View Farm
Westerdale
Westerdale Hall
Hall Farm
Riddings Farm
extension B
Daleside Farm
Grange Farm
Hawthorn House Farm
Stocking House
Start
To Kildale
New House Farm
Wood End Farm
Waites House Farm
Westerdale Moor
N
0
0
1 kilometre
1 mile
ruin
Esklets
To Farndale

WESTERDALE

WALK 25

★

Main walk 5½ miles (9 km)
Extension A adds 3 miles (5 km); extension B adds a further
5 miles (8 km) to Esklets or 6½ miles (10 km) to the old railway
(part of this extension is an 'out and in', using the same path
on the outward and return journeys).

Westerdale is the valley of the river Esk from its source high on
Westerdale Moor to where it turns east near Castleton. The main walk
explores the lower part of the valley, extension A takes in the subsidiary
valley of Tower Beck to the east, and extension B enables you to visit the
headwaters of the Esk and to climb up to the old railway on the watershed
for a view down into Farndale. That, by the way, is also the start of the
Esk Valley Walk, which follows the river from its source to the sea, and
today's ramble with extension B takes in the whole of the first 5 miles of
that walk (its logo is a leaping fish, which you will see frequently on
signposts and waymarks). Westerdale deserves a long day of leisurely
exploration, with the variety of its landscapes, one as beautiful as the
other, and its glorious views. The suggested walk is a long one, but a
good part of it is on quiet tarmac lanes.

Driving on the narrow moorland road from Kildale to Westerdale,
having passed the popular picnic spot at Hob Hole (the start of Walk 26),
crossed the ford and climbed the steep hill, take the first, minor road on
the right (John Breckon Road on the map) and drive along it for about
600 yards until a wall comes close to the road on the left; here there is
a layby for several cars (made for the use of those shooting from the butts
up on the moor). Park here (GR 654 065).

Walk back along the way you have just come, passing a bridleway sign
on the left which is followed on Walk 26. You are already on the route
of the Esk Valley Walk, as the wooden signpost at the next junction
confirms. Turn right up the main road. Just over the brow of the hill a
green footpath signpost points half-left over Westerdale Moor. Now
follows the only section of our walk where the route is not clear on the
ground, but it is very short. Look across the moor in the exact direction
indicated by the signpost: for the first few yards there is no clear path, but
then you will notice a thin break through the heather. Follow this, and
when the heather thins out keep on in the same direction — there are
shooting butts over to your left — and once you cross the crest of the moor
you will see a footpath signpost ahead, and your difficulties are over.

Having reached the signpost, follow the direction indicated — downhill towards a wall. Past a cairn the path is slightly clearer, and soon it bears left and you are walking parallel to the wall and some 20 yards from it. The path leads into a hollow way which bears slightly right down towards Dale View Farm. Pass a marker post and keep downhill close to the wall to pass through a gate into a pasture. Keep slanting downhill towards the house, join the tarmac access road and bear left along it. It soon deteriorates into a track; keep on along this, bearing right with it to a gate. Having passed through the gate the track forks: ignore the branch going left and keep forward down to another signposted gate. Turn left between walls to another large gate and follow the track forward with a wall to your left to another waymarked gate.

The track continues, now with a wall to the right, and leads through another gate. When the wall on your right turns sharp right, keep forward to a gateway at the end of the wall on the left, go through and turn sharp left, but where the wall on your left turns sharp left, turn sharp right, following the old field boundary on your right to a gate in the wall ahead, which leads you out on to the moor again. Follow the wall on your right, but where it goes right and then left again, your path cuts the corner. There is a lovely view down towards Castleton. Soon there is a steep valley in front of you and the path drops into it, a particularly lovely section which leads to a footbridge by which we cross the Esk for the first time.

Keep forward up the slope on the grassy path through bracken to a signpost. Here we leave the Esk Valley Walk, which goes left, by bearing right up a clear grassy path. At the motor road cross diagonally left to find the continuation of the grassy path, now a grassy track slanting right up through the bracken. When the path forks keep left, still up the slope, parallel to a wall on the right. When the wall bears off right, keep on up the clear path, with a glorious view right and back. The grassy path leads to a road: cross straight over and walk forward the 20 odd yards to another road, along which you turn right.

There are lovely views right over Westerdale. Follow the road until you are just opposite the second of two farms close together down on the right, where a minor tarmac lane forks right. The main walk follows this, **extension A** keeps straight on along the road (see [†] below). Pass through two gates and ignore a track forking right to Quarry Farm. The narrow ribbon of tarmac drops to an attractive ford and bridge over Tower Beck, an obvious spot for a picnic, before climbing to a crossroads. Keep straight ahead to the next T-junction and turn right through Westerdale village. Move to [#] below.

[†] **For extension A** keep straight on along the road. At the next fork the right branch leads to Brown Hill House Farm, but we keep left uphill. When you reach the main road, coming up over Castleton Rigg from Castleton, bear right along it. Danby Botton is down to your left (see Walk 24).

Opposite the next road junction, where a minor road drops sharp left to Danby Botton, follow the public bridleway sign pointing back right along a clear path through the heather. From the edge of the escarpment, where you again have a fine view over the valley of Tower Beck, the path slants down the hillside then makes for Dale Head Farm. Pass through a gate and down into the yard to a large tree, where you bear sharp left to a gate between buildings, then right downhill, with the farm buildings to your right. When the track forks keep right, down to pass through the right-hand of two gates, then follow the track with a wall to your left. Pass through a gateway and head downhill, still beside the wall. At the bottom of the field the path bears right downhill into the wooded valley of Tower Beck, a lovely spot.

Cross the beck by the bridge, pass through the gate and bear very slightly right up the track across the field to a stile by a gate in the wall ahead. The clear track now has a wall to the left. Go through another gate, and now the wall is to your right. Pass through two more gates and walk straight through the yard at Broad Gate Farm and on along the tarmac lane (Broad Gate Road). At the point where the lane passes through a gateway, a yard or two to the left, in the wall, there is a broken stone step-stile: cross this and bear half-left across the field to the next stile a yard or two to the left of a telegraph pole. Over this very fine stone stepladder stile keep your direction over the next field to a gate. Through this walk straight across the next field to another gate and out on to the road. Here you turn left and rejoin the route of the main walk. At the next T-junction turn right through Westerdale village.

[#] **To continue the main walk** take the minor road on the left shortly after passing the church, a no through road [for **extension B** move to [*] below]. The road swings right and then left again past Westerdale Hall, a Victorian shooting lodge of the Duncombe family which used to be a youth hostel. Pass Hall Farm, ignoring a road forking right past the front of the farmhouse, and follow the road along and down to recross the Esk. Shortly after it bears sharp right up towards the moor, ignore an access track on the right to Grange Farm, and follow it up to a gate. Here a fish signpost indicates that you are rejoining the Esk Valley Walk, and here too you are joined by walkers who have done Extension B. The main track turns left, but you turn right along the grassy track. Move to final paragraph.

[*] **Extension B**. Enter the main gate of the church, rebuilt in the 19th century, and bear left along the side of it. Just before you reach the door into the church at the far end, bear half-left across the churchyard to a small gate near the far corner. Now bear slightly right downhill through the trees, cross a beck and pass through another small gate, cross another beck and bear half-left up the slope. A clear path leads forward, parallel to the beck down on your left. When you are faced by another small gate, don't go through, but bear slightly right and follow the fence on your left round. The clear path leads forward to a gate in a corner where a fence

on the left meets a wall on the right. Pass through and follow the wall on your right until you meet a tarmac road.

Bear right along the tarmac road and follow it until a notice warns you of a ford; here the road drops and forks: keep left across the ford (or footbridge). A short distance further ignore a track forking right down to Wood End Farm and pass through a gateway, where the lane forks again: the left branch leads to Waites House Farm, you go right and the tarmac ends. Follow the track, passing through a gate, then bearing right and descending to the river. You cross the footbridge on your return route, but now follow the signpost saying 'Footpath to Farndale', which points back left, parallel to the river.

Soon you are following a wall/fence on the left and the clear path leads along to a step-stile in a facing wall. Continue along the top of the bank, soon with a fence to your right. Go through a gate in the next facing wall and keep on along the path, still with the fence/wall to your right (don't be tempted to fork left up the hillside). When the wall ends, with the infant river in a steep ravine some distance to your right, keep forward along the clear path. Parts can be very wet, as it is crossed by a number of becks coming down the slope, and at these points the route of the path may briefly be unclear; but keep forward and you will soon pick it up again. Soon after you reach white paint waymarks on rocks the path drops to cross the beck by a footbridge.

The clear path continues forward from the bridge then bears right up the slope, then left to a stile in a wall. Continue along the clear path, soon passing through a gate, from where you have a fence to your right. But shortly you bear slightly left away from the fence (a marker post shows you the direction) with the track, through a gateway in a facing wall, and now there is a wall to your left. Follow the track through the ruins of Esklets Farm and along to a ford over a beck. The headwaters of the Esk flow down the valleys all around you. If you want to continue up to the watershed, simply follow the very good track up the slope on your right until you reach the old railway, then return by the same route.

From Esklets return by your outward route to the ford, footbridge and signpost to Farndale. Cross the bridge and turn right (Esk Valley Walk signpost to Castleton) with the beck to your right. The path leads to a white footbridge, from which you keep straight forward towards Wood End Farm. Cross a beck and stile and pass to the left of all the buildings, then bear slightly right to a gate, and through this turn sharp left and walk straight across the next large pasture to a stile in what from a distance looks like a wooden gate. From this stile again keep straight forward, cross over a farm access track, and follow the line of overhead wires to a stile in the wall ahead in the field corner. Keep the beck down on your right to the next stile, then walk straight across the next field to the next stile, which you will already see, a yard or two to the right of a power line pole. Cross the stile/footbridge/stile, from which a very clear grassy path leads forward. Cross a beck by stepping-stones, and with New House Farm up to your left follow the clear path up to a gate. Turn right along the track and follow it until it turns right through a gate. At this point you rejoin the route of the main walk. Don't go through the gate, but keep straight forward along the grassy track.

Continuing the main walk the moor is to your left and a wall to your right. When you reach a fork, keep left with the main track, climbing slightly. Pass through a waymarked gate in the wall ahead into an enclosed pasture. Keep along the edge of the field, pass through a gateway and continue, still with a wall on your right, to a waymarked gate in the far corner. Now there is no track. The right of way swings very slightly right, then very slightly left again, heading towards Hawthorn House Farm. Having crossed a beck you are back on a track which leads to a gate to the left of the farm buildings. Keep forward through the yard, then bear slightly left on to the farm access road. Having crossed a wooded beck and passed through a gateway, the track forks: keep left. The track climbs well to the left of Stocking House and passes through a gate on to the open moor. Here the tarmac begins again, and it is only a short distance to the car.

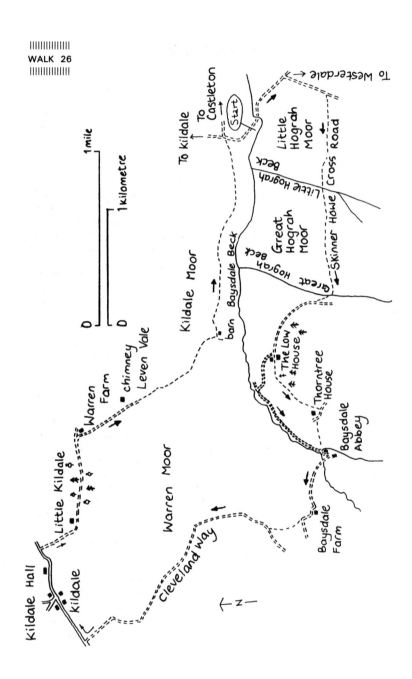

BAYSDALE

WALK 26

★

8 miles (12.5 km)

A fine moorland tramp on clear paths leads to a secluded and very lovely valley with a large mansion built on the site of a medieval Cistercian nunnery, then the Cleveland Way is followed to the village of Kildale, where refreshments are available, and finally good paths lead past an old ironstone mine and over Kildale Moor back into Baysdale, where a clear moorland path is followed back to the starting point.

Park the car at Hob Hole, which lies in Baysdale on the narrow motor road between Kildale and Westerdale, a popular picnic place near a water splash and footbridge. There is plenty of room on the sheep-cropped turf (GR 652 074).

Leave the car park, cross the footbridge and walk steeply uphill on the road. When you reach an unsignposted road junction, fork right along the minor road (John Breckon Road) and follow it up and over the crest, from where there is a lovely view over Westerdale, and on until you reach a signposted bridleway on the right. Follow this clear path through the heather, at first roughly parallel to a line of shooting butts over to the left. You are now crossing Little Hograh Moor by the old Skinner Howe Cross Road. The cairned path eventually leads down into a shallow dip, where you cross the infant Little Hograh Beck, and then up over Great Hograh Moor. Just before you descend into the next dip there is a memorial on a cairned rock on the right to Alan Clegg, who loved these moors. There is a delightful bridge over Great Hograh Beck, which tumbles over rocks and is tree-lined from here to Baysdale Beck. Ignore the path steeply up the bank ahead and bear right, at first parallel to the beck but soon bearing gently away from it over the moor. Soon you join a broader track coming over your left shoulder and follow it until it leads to the right of a conifer plantation and to a gate. Keep on downhill with the wood to your left and a wall to your right to The Low House.

(**Please note**: A proposal is currently being considered to change the route of the right of way between The Low House and Baysdale Abbey. I have described the path as it is at present, but please keep a look out for signs that it has been diverted. The new route, if accepted, will lead down the track from The Low House to Baysdale Beck, there turning left to follow the beck to Baysdale Abbey — see the sketch map.)

Pass through the gate and bear slightly right through the yard, with the house to your left and a barn on the right, to a waymarked stile on the far side leading into a wood. Walk down with a wall to your right, crossing two tracks which lead through gates in this wall, and now you are climbing, still between the wood and the wall. Leave the wood through a gate and keep following the wall on your right towards the next gate. A few yards to the left of this gate, near the wall corner, there is a step-stile. Cross this, and now the wall is to your left. Pass through the gate in the far corner of this field, and keep on by the wall to a gate in the far corner of the next field.

Through the gate, bear slightly right — Thorntree House is down on your right — towards the bottom corner of the larch wood ahead, but before you reach it you meet a track coming down the slope. Turn right down it, and bear left to a gate just to the left of a small outbuilding. Walk forward a few yards more on the track, but where it curves right down by the wall, keep straight forward diagonally down the field to the bottom end of the wall on the far side, crossing several wet channels on the way. Where the wall joins the fence there is a gate: pass through and bear half-right down the slope towards a bridge over Baysdale Beck. Cross the bridge and bear left with the track through the yard of Baysdale Abbey.

Before the large house bear right along the access road, through the gateposts, over the bridge and up to pass to the right of the buildings of Baysdale Farm. When the road makes a sharp left-hand bend, keep straight forward up the slope on a reasonable path with a wall to your right. Pause at the top for breath and to admire the lovely view back over Baysdale, then go through the gate in the corner and bear very very slightly right up a clear narrow path across the moor. Higher up you may be confused by a variety of paths, but keep your direction upwards and at the top you will rejoin the tarmac road (and join the Cleveland Way, which has come over from Bloworth Crossing).

The view is superb, from Captain Cook's Monument and Roseberry Topping to Middlesborough and over the Cleveland Plain to the distant Pennines. It will compensate for a longish stretch on tarmac, as you bear right along the road and follow it all the way down to the motor road on the outskirts of Kildale. Here turn right to the village and walk through it, ignoring roads on the left to the station (here the Cleveland Way leaves you to climb to Captain Cook's Monument) and passing the Victorian Kildale Hall on the left.

Take the first minor road on the right, a no through road signposted to 'Little Kildale'. After passing the cottages there the road climbs through Little Kildale Wood. Near the top of the wood the road forks and a public bridleway sign points you to the left. This metalled track leads to Warren Farm, just before which you bear right along a signposted fenced track which leads to the right of the farm and a narrow wood to a gate. Keep on the track downhill, passing to the right of a large brick chimney and the remains of the Leven Vale ironstone drift mine (from which a railway formerly ran to link with the Eskdale line), cross the beck and pass through a gate, after which the track leads up through some trees to another gate.

Now bear slightly right, over to the fence, and follow it up to another gate out on to Kildale Moor. A narrow path continues forward up the slope, clear after the first few yards, and leads to a gate in a cross wall at the top of the moor. The view back is extensive. A clear path continues forward through the heather. Pass a marker post and a cairn, and soon Baysdale lies at your feet, with your outward route clear on the other side. The path is now heading down to a stone barn with some ruined buildings beyond it. Turn left in front of the barn along a broad path and follow it all the way back along the valley side to the motor road, where you turn right downhill to return to the car.

DANBY BEACON

★

6 miles (9.5 km)

Today's objective offers probably the best all round viewpoint in the National Park north of the river Esk. Although it is easily reached by car it is situated in good walking country, worth combining with a visit to the lovely riverside village of Lealholm, our chosen starting point. Lealholm can be reached from the Whitby to Guisborough road via Stonegate or by minor roads from Danby or Glaisdale. A roomy car park and toilets are provided near the village green by the river (GR 763 076).

Explore the village before setting out. A bridge crosses the wide rippling river. On the south side are picnic areas and an inn; on the north, a war memorial and an Edwardian drinking fountain (not in use) with a substantial iron drinking cup still firmly chained to the stonework.

The walk has been devised to include the trim village of Houlsyke, but to avoid tarmac roads as much as possible. Those who do not wish to follow the detailed field route, where close attention must be paid to finding the correct way, could take the low road out of Lealholm, picking up the trail at Houlsyke; or if you would prefer a high level road, missing that village, take the uphill road from the car park, passing the 'suburb' of Lealholmside, turn left at the road junction above, bear left at the next fork and keep to the tarmac road for about 1½ miles, looking out for the gate over the minor road on the left coming up from Houlsyke. Turn right and follow the route from [*] below.

Field walkers turn uphill from the car park, cross over the railway and turn left immediately; just past the station building fork right uphill on a grassy track through a gate. Immediately before the next pair of facing gates bear right off the track along with a wall to your left to a footpath sign which you can see at the far end of the wall. Here go through the gate on the left and bear half-right over the field, following the direction to Houlsyke via Hole-i'-th'-Ellers, to a stile 5 yards to the right of a metal gate on the far side. Keep forward with a hedge to your right; in the far corner of the field cross the stile on the right and bear left following the hedge on your left. Cross a step-stile in a cross wall and continue with the fence to your left, following it round until you come to a stile by a large gate. Now bear half-right across the next large field, all the time approaching the wood on your left, and heading to the far left-hand corner, where there is a stile by a gate. Cross a beck to another gate, then continue the line of the short lane you have just been in up the facing

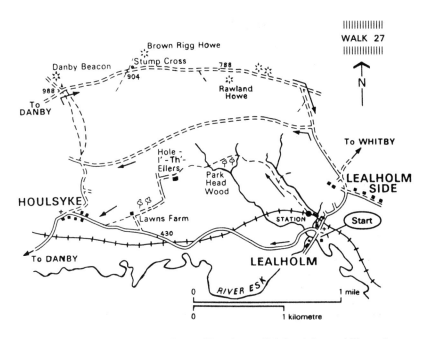

hillside to a stile in a facing fence. Now bear slightly right, uphill, and when you reach the brow you will see that you are making for a stile by a gate in the fence/wall ahead.

Cross the stile and bear left on the track, which soon bears right, round the edge of the field. Keep along the field edge, follow the wall on your left through a gap and on to the abandoned farm of Hole-i'-th'-Ellers. The path passes behind, i.e. to the right of the buildings, to a stile by a gate. Keep forward along the edge of the field with a wall to your right to a stile by the gate in the next corner then turn sharp left down with the wall to your left. When the wall turns left keep straight ahead down the track, which bears left near the foot of the field to a gate just to the right of a ruined building. Cross the step-stile by the gate, ignore the gateway to your left and keep forward with a wall to your left. Cross another step-stile and keep the wall to your left, pass through a gap in a facing wall and walk straight over the next field to a facing gap to the left of a small wood, with the buildings of Lawns Farm beyond. At the end of the wood cross the stile by the gate and walk forward to another gate into the farmyard.

Keep ahead through the farmyard, bearing left in it on to the access road, leave it by a gate and a few yards further on go through a gate in the fence on the right and walk along the edge of the field with the hedge/wall to your right. Cross the stile in the far corner under a power line pole and continue across the next field to a gate on the far side. Cut the corner of the next field to a gate out on to the road and bear right

87

along this to Houlsyke. Halfway through the village turn acutely right on a narrow tarmac road where a sign shows the gradient to be one in four. Keep going uphill, ignoring a road to the right (to Hollins Farm) and enjoying the glorious view back. Pass through a gate onto a cross road.

[*] Cross straight over the road and up the hollow way through the bracken, an old 'county road' across the moor. There is a plethora of paths, but in a few yards you will see the trig point and the cross on Danby Beacon, and that is your objective. Following a line of shooting butts is helpful; when they end you don't have much further to go and a way can be picked through the heather. From the Beacon the course of the river Esk from west to east can be traced, together with the valleys of its tributaries, notably Great and Little Fryup Dales, comprehensively viewed from this point. The distinctive Easby Moor is away to the west, but weather conditions would have to be particularly clear to see the Captain Cook Monument on its top. In the north-west, peeping over the line of Danby Low Moor, is Freebrough Hill; it is only 821 feet high but its conical shape is well known to motorists making for Whitby from Teesside, as is also Scaling Dam, the stretch of water seen to the north of the Beacon, two miles away.

Do not be deterred by the mileage shown on the guidepost to Lealholm: the direct route which we shall take is much shorter! The track is a delight to follow, particularly when the heather is in bloom. After half a mile, just after a cross track marked by bridleway signs, look left for Stump Cross. At the first major fork in the track, with a public bridleway sign on the left, go right, soon to join the tarmac road which may have been chosen by some for the outward route. Join the main road where a sign shows Ugthorpe and Whitby to the left, Lealholm and Rosedale to the right. Go downhill past Lealholmside to the starting point.

HIGHCLIFF NAB

WALK 28

★

4 miles (6.5 km)

On the road between Commondale and Kildale there is a crossroads at which the road going south-east is signposted to Westerdale and the road going north-west is unsignposted: take this road and follow it to where the tarmac ends at the far corner of a wood. Park here (GR 606 118).

The first stretch of the walk is shared with Walk 29. Walk along the track which continues the line of the tarmac road, a sandy track signposted public bridleway. This is the Percy Cross Rigg road. The wooded hill over to your right is Highcliff Nab, the goal of today's walk, with

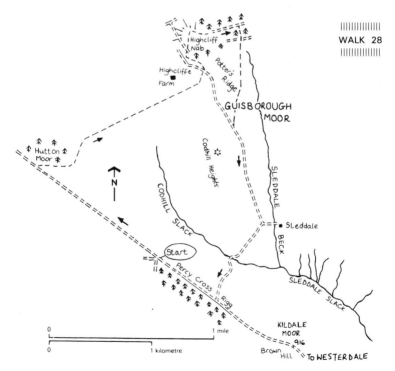

WALK 28

89

Highcliffe Farm in the middle of its green fields in front. When you reach a building which was once an old air raid shelter or ammunition store there is a fine view over Guisborough to the sea. About 150 yards before you reach the next forest fork right on a clear path slanting back through the heather signposted Cleveland Way.

The path soon leads along the boundary wall of the fields of Highcliffe Farm. When you reach the trees look back for a view to the Captain Cook Monument, then go through the gate (Cleveland Way sign) and follow the clear path forward through the wood. After keeping along the outside edge of the wood for a short distance the track bears right. Cross a forest road, climb a few steps and continue on the ascending path through the bracken. Soon you must bear right up some more steps to the summit of the Nab. The view is extensive, dominated by Guisborough below.

Leave the Nab along the narrow path with the steep drop to your left. When you reach a forest road turn left along it, but at the next junction fork right, leaving the Cleveland Way. In 150 yards you leave the forest through a gate, cross over a grassy track and follow the narrow trod straight ahead through the heather. The farm ahead in the dip surrounded by its green fields is Sleddale. The path passes the right-hand end of a line of shooting butts. The heather is sometimes quite deep, but the path is usually clear. When you reach a broad track bear left along it, passing well to the right of Sleddale Farm. At the T-junction by the wood turn right along the tarmac road to return to the car.

CAPTAIN COOK MONUMENT AND ROSEBERRY TOPPING

WALK 29

★

6½ miles (10.5 km)

In some of the most dramatic parts of the National Park, today's journey makes an ideal walk. All the tracks are well marked, if sometimes muddy, and there is something of everything — good shapes, steep cliffs, pastoral valleys and heather moors.

The most accessible starting point for the simple climb of Roseberry Topping — 1,051 feet above sea level but looking higher because of its conical shape — is the lane just south of the village of Newton under Roseberry, which is a little over a mile north of Great Ayton. This is the point used by the White Rose walkers as the beginning of the 34 or 40 mile journey along the tops to the White Horse at Kilburn. The views of the Cleveland Plain from the rocky top are splendid, the patchwork quilt effect being particularly marked in the fields at harvest time when, in late August, the moorland heather should also be at its best.

The starting point for the round trip now proposed is however to be Gribdale Gate, where there is accommodation for many cars. To reach it take the road towards Little Ayton out of Great Ayton, turning left on the outskirts for the railway station, and continuing forward as far as the cattle grid at the top, 750 feet above sea level. Park either before or after the cattle grid (GR 592 110).

Go through the gate into the Cleveland Forest (signposted Cleveland Way: Kildale) and follow the broad track up to the Captain Cook Monument. Captain Cook spent his youth at Easby, down below, and went to school in Great Ayton. The memorial is of 'the celebrated circumnavigator Captain James Cook, FRS, a man in nautical knowledge inferior to none . . .' There is a splendid view to the south of the 'bumps' of Hasty Bank, Cold Moor, Cringle Moor and beyond.

From the monument take the obvious green track through the heather (again signposted Cleveland Way: Kildale) to the corner of the wood and pass through the gap in the wall. The monument is on Easby Moor; now we move onto Coate Moor, on a good track with a larch wood on the left. Ahead, slightly to the right, is Kildale in the valley of the river Leven. At a major fork keep right, along the branch which keeps closer to the steep drop on the right, and follow this track, which can be wet in places, until it joins a forest road (by a Cleveland Way sign), along which you bear

91

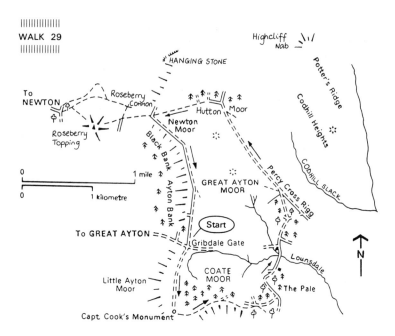

right. On reaching a tarred byroad you turn left, leaving the Cleveland Way.

The road passes downhill into Lounsdale (incorrectly 'Lonsdale' on some maps), beautifully green among the bracken covered hills and the forests on the other side. Pass Lounsdale Farm and drop to cross Lounsdale Beck. Immediately after some barns on the left the tarmac road turns left, and this would be a short-cut back to the car, but we keep straight on through a gate and uphill on a stony track towards the wood. When you reach the trees you join a forest track coming in from the right, bear left and continue up, at first just inside the forest boundary, but soon climbing quite steeply through the forest. Ignoring minor tracks to right and left you leave the forest through a large wooden gate and reach the end of a tarmac road coming up from the right (the starting point for Walk 28).

Looking left there are several tracks: you want to follow the one which continues the line of the tarmac road, a sandy track signposted 'Public Bridleway'. This is the Percy Cross Rigg road. When you reach a building which was once an old air raid shelter or ammunition store there is a fine view over Guisborough to the sea. As you approach the next forest the Cleveland Way comes in from the right. Pass through the gate into the forest and immediately turn left (Cleveland Way sign) on the track along the edge of the trees. After some distance you must ignore two right forks down into the forest in quick succession, but a few yards further on you leave the forest by a gate on the left (Cleveland Way sign)

92

and take the clear track across the moor. When you breast the brow, the tip of the Topping comes into sight. Keep forward to a gate in the wall beside another section of forest.

Pass through the gate (signposted Roseberry Topping). Soon you will see the sharp drop of 200 feet to Roseberry Common and a rise of 200 feet to the summit; the path is good all the way and you will be well rewarded when you have made the climb. Then you must return the same way to the corner gate! Now follow the signpost 'Cleveland Way: Gribdale Gate' on a clear track with the wall and wood to your right; it leads back to the car.

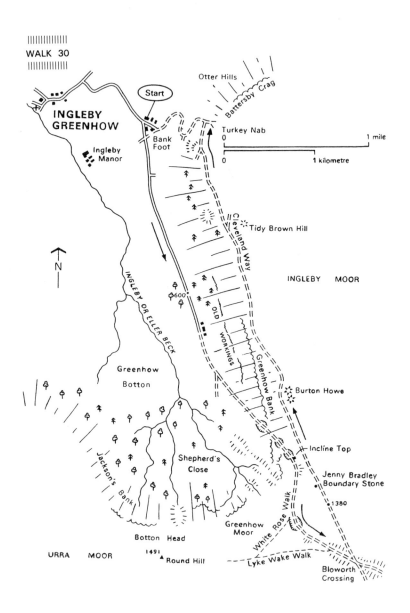

WALK 30

INGLEBY GREENHOW

Start

Ingleby Manor

Bank Foot

Otter Hills

Battersby Crag

Turkey Nab

0   1 mile

0   1 kilometre

Tidy Brown Hill

Cleveland Way

600

OLD

WORKINGS

INGLEBY   MOOR

N

INGLEBY OR ELLER BECK

Greenhow Bottom

Greenhow Bank

Burton Howe

Incline Top

Jenny Bradley Boundary Stone

Shepherd's Close

Jackson's Bank

1380

White Rose Walk

Greenhow Moor

Botton   Head

URRA   MOOR   1491 ▲ Round Hill

Lyke Wake Walk

Bloworth Crossing

GREENHOW BOTTON
AND BLOWORTH CROSSING

WALK 30

★

7½ miles (12 km)

This final chapter is a link with the first of these two books, North Yorks Moors Walks for Motorists (West and South), taking the reader back to the watershed which in these parts divides the two volumes. On the way out we use the track of the old Rosedale Railway, built in 1861 to transport iron ore from the mines at Rosedale to the blast furnaces of Teesside and which at the Ingleby Incline climbs diagonally up the escarpment, rising nearly 700 feet in little more than a mile. The return will be on the famous moorland road from Kirkbymoorside and Rudland Rigg.

Ingleby Greenhow is one of the many lovely villages beautifully situated below the escarpment of the Cleveland Hills near Stokesley. Motoring towards it from any direction is a pleasure: from Helmsley through Bilsdale; from Thirsk, turning off the Stokesley road near Carlton; or from Stokesley, Great Ayton or Kildale. A quarter of a mile out of the village on the road to Battersby and Kildale take the turning to Bank Foot, parking the car where the road forks just before the farm (GR 592 061). Here you will see a sign 'Footpath to the Incline' and another 'No admittance to unauthorized vehicles'. Following both instructions on the good surface of the old railway track, opportunity may be taken to step out and at the same time to take stock of the surroundings.

On the immediate right are the grounds of Ingleby Manor, former home of the Sidney family, Lords De L'isle and Dudley; in the background are the famous bumps of Hasty Bank, Cold Moor and Cringle Moor. The valley ahead is Greenhow Botton — Botton being a Scandinavian word for a rounded valley — scooped out and typically glacial. Having gone through the gate just after four ex-railway cottages, keep left at the next fork to climb the Incline. Keep on the track after it levels out at the top, and follow it to where there are two gates across it about 200 yards apart: the second of these is at Bloworth Crossing.

Here turn left, following the route of the Cleveland Way. The first item of interest is the Jenny Bradley Boundary Stone, where a tall stone marked F (for Feversham) and dated 1888 stands alongside the older cross in its stone socket. A good way further on you pass Burton (or Botton) Howe, a tumulus to the right of the track, and after a fairly long stretch where the track is quite close to the edge of the escarpment there is another guidestone about 30 yards to the right of the track with directions to Kirby (Moorside), He(l)msley, Stoxley and Gisboro.

About 200 yards after passing a low stone on the left marked Greenhow Road the track forks: there are two gates on the right and a Cleveland Way sign on the left pointing along the right-hand branch. We take the left fork, i.e. continue straight forward. Our road soon loses height until at a corner a fine scene reveals itself: the Captain Cook Monument and Roseberry Topping will have been seen for some time ahead, but now they make a splendid backcloth to the vale of the river Leven, which flows below Easby Moor on which the Cook Monument stands. The village below is Battersby, the terrace of houses to the left being Battersby Junction. Away to the right, below the nab, is Kildale. Now wind your way downhill and you will soon be back at Bank Foot.